101 Questions & Answers on

THE SACRAMENTS OF HEALING

101 Questions & Answers on THE SACRAMENTS OF HEALING

Penance and Anointing of the Sick

Paul Jerome Keller, OP

Paulist Press
New York/Mahwah, NJ

Nihil Obstat:
Giles Dimock, OP, STD
Censor Deputatus

Imprimi potest:
Dominic Izzo, OP
Prior Provincial, St. Joseph Province Order of Preachers

January 12, 2010

Cover design by Sharyn Banks
Book design by Lynn Else

Library of Congress Cataloging-in-Publication Data

Keller, Paul Jerome.
101 questions & answers on the sacraments of healing : penance and anointing of the sick / Paul Jerome Keller.
p. cm.
Includes bibliogrphical references (p.) and index.
ISBN 978-0-8091-4660-4 (alk. paper)
1. Penance—Miscellanea. 2. Extreme unction—Miscellanea. 3. Catholic Church—Doctrines—Miscellanea. I. Title. II. Title: 101 questions and answers on the sacraments of healing.
BX2260.K39 2010
264′.02086—dc22

2009048426

Published by Paulist Press
997 Macarthur Boulevard
Mahwah, New Jersey 07430

www.paulistpress.com

Printed and bound in the
United States of America

Contents

B. The Sickness of Sin

C. Conversion and Penance: An Age-Old Remedy

D. The Priest as the Minister of Penance

E. The Rite of Penance

Dedicated to
Our Lady of Guadalupe, Patroness of the Americas,
and to
Dominic Aquinas Gondreau

When I declared not my sin, my body wasted away
through my groaning all day long.
Psalm 32:3, RSV

The LORD…heals the brokenhearted,
and binds up their wounds.
Psalm 147:3

Preface

It had been my original intention to write a book on the sacrament of penance by itself. There has been a great need for a work that would be both substantial in terms of content as well as intelligible to the relative newcomer to the theology of the sacrament. It was the excellent idea of my editor, Nancy de Flon, to treat both of the sacraments of healing—penance and the anointing of the sick—as part of the Paulist Press 101 Questions and Answers series. The number *101* may be deceptive: in no way does this exhaust the treatment of these sacraments. Indeed, it is only a beginning. I have tried to include as many questions as possible, from both the lay and the priestly perspectives, drawing on my work as a parish priest at St. Mary's Church in New Haven, Connecticut, as well as on other pastoral and academic experience afforded me as a Dominican priest and teacher of theology. Thus, I believe that this little summary of many key points concerning these two sacraments will be quite useful to a number of people: laymen and laywomen, religious education instructors, RCIA instructors and students, college students, seminarians, and priests. May we all grow in our knowledge and love of these two instruments given us by Christ, fruits of his passion to make us whole: "By his wounds you have been healed" (1 Pet 2:24).

I owe a debt of gratitude to a number of my brothers in the Province of St. Joseph of the Order of Preachers whose support, be it moral, spiritual, or material, has helped to bring this project to its completion. Two professors deserve to be singled out: Fr. (now Archbishop) Augustine DiNoia, OP (now Secretary of the Vatican Congregation for Divine Worship and the Discipline of the Sacraments); and Fr. Romanus Cessario, OP, for having provided a firm foundation in my theological education. I thank, as well, the brethren at Providence College where this book began, especially Fr. John Vidmar, OP, and the brothers at St. Dominic Priory, where it was completed. I am especially grateful for the encouragement of Fr. James M. Sullivan, OP, my prior, and Fr. Chris Saliga, OP, RN; and for the help of Fr. Giles Dimock, OP. Ever supportive, even while busy about his studies in Fribourg, Switzerland, was Fr. Dominic M. Langevin, OP, whom I cannot thank enough. Providence College professor of theology Paul Gondreau, PhD, deserves great gratitude as well. I also thank Fr. Dominic D. Izzo, OP, my prior provincial. All the prayers of the nuns at the Dominican Monastery in Buffalo and the Pittsford Carmel and many other friends were key to completing this work. Finally, again special gratitude goes to Nancy de Flon, my editor, whose assistance was invaluable. Grazie mille a tutti!

Paul Jerome Keller, OP
Solemnity of the Most Holy Trinity
June 7, 2009

List of Abbreviations

AAS	*Acta Apostolicae Sedis.*
CIC	*Codex Iuris Canonici.* The Code of Canon Law, 1983.
CCC	*Catechism of the Catholic Church.* USCC, 1997.
RC	*Reconciliatio et Paenitentia.* On Reconciliation and Penance. John Paul II, 1984.
RP	*The Rite of Penance.*
PCS	*Pastoral Care of the Sick: Rites of Anointing and Viaticum.*
SC	*Sacrosanctum Concilium.* The Constitution on the Sacred Liturgy, 1963.
SCar	*Sacramentum Caritatis.* Apostolic Exhortation on the Eucharist. Benedict XVI, 2007.
ST	*Summa Theologiae* of St. Thomas Aquinas, OP.
SUI	*Sacram Unctionem Infirmorum.* Apostolic Constitution. Paul VI, 1972.

PART ONE

The Sacraments of Healing in General

1. Aren't all the sacraments healing?

It is true that all seven sacraments can be said to have the power to heal. This is because the sacraments were given to us by Christ to perpetuate the healing he came to bring to all people. Of course, to speak of healing is to presuppose a sickness. In this case, the root of the sickness is the sin of our first parents, Adam and Eve. By rebelling against God, they exposed themselves to a malady with no known cure among humanity, a spiritual cancer that could only end in death.

However, God would not be frustrated in his desire that his beloved human sons and daughters share in the communion of his divine, trinitarian life. The scriptures reveal the plan God used to heal and restore us to life, culminating in his Son becoming a man so that we might share in his divinity.

The healing that Christ would bring is prefigured many times in the Old Testament, but a most apt image is found in the Book of Numbers. The Israelites were dying as a result of being bitten by seraph serpents. Once they repented of their rebellion, God offered them a very specific healing. Moses was to make a bronze image of the seraph serpent and mount it on a pole. Whoever had been bitten by a serpent had only to look at the bronze image to be healed (Num 21:4–9). This instance of healing is fulfilled in Jesus, as he himself tells us: "And just as Moses lifted up the serpent in the wilderness, so must the Son of Man be lifted up, that whoever believes in him may have eternal life" (John 3:14–15). Christ crucified and risen from the dead is our healing from the poisonous bite of sin.

The sacraments are the continuation of Christ's healing, even as he now sits at the right hand of the Father. They are the divine prescriptions made to all people of all places in all times to heal the deadly effects of sin. Hugh of St. Victor, a medieval theologian, explained that the sacraments are spiritual medicines that, though applied externally to our bodies, heal our souls by means of invisible truth. The sacraments, he said, are the medicines for the soul that, when administered properly, cause the wounds of our souls to be cured; and, being "cured and healed we may be able to attain to the promise of perpetual life."

St. Thomas Aquinas (1225–74) likewise spoke about all the sacraments as having been instituted by Christ as remedies for the defects arising from sin. He saw the sacraments as having a supernatural correspondence with various aspects of natural life. In baptism, we are reborn into a new life with Christ; in confirmation, the Holy Spirit strengthens us still further; in the Eucharist, we receive help to fight against temptation; in penance, we are healed from the actual sins committed after baptism; in the anointing of the sick, we receive a balm for the remainders of sin; and so forth (*ST* III, q. 65, a. 1).

2. Why do we speak about penance and anointing in particular as healing sacraments?

When the sacraments heal us, they restore us to life and make it possible for us to worship God more perfectly. Nevertheless, two of the sacraments in particular have a healing character about them. In explaining this, St. Thomas Aquinas draws an analogy between bodily and spiritual health, noting that just as a person suffers from physical weakness so, too, he or she may suffer from spiritual weakness. There are two ways to heal someone. One way is to strike at the heart of the sickness. We might think of surgery or a medical treatment as ways of doing this. Spiritually speaking, this amounts to the sacrament of penance. It restores health to the soul immediately by the forgiveness of sins. The other way to help someone return to physical health, according to St. Thomas, is to give him or her a proper diet and exercise. The sacrament of the anointing of the sick accomplishes this in the spiritual life because it provides the grace needed for a person to be spiritually strong in the midst of illness; furthermore, it removes sin and makes the person ready for the beatific vision when it is time to pass from this life (*ST* III, q. 65, a. 1).

3. Why have a separate book on just these two sacraments instead of treating the healing power of all the sacraments?

While all the sacraments offer healing in some way, penance and anointing have unique roles as extensions of Christ's healing power through the Holy Spirit. Far from being superfluous, these two sacraments give Christians a privileged opportunity to deepen in friendship with God precisely in those moments of brokenness and frailty caused by sin and illness. They are the continuation of the mercy of Jesus, who will not abandon us even in the darkest moments of life. He tells us that he came to invite, not the self-righteous to a change of heart, but sinners. For "those who are well have no need of a physician, but those who are sick; I have come to call not the righteous but sinners to repentance" (Luke 5:31–32). Jesus Christ is the Divine Physician who desires to heal in us what has been destroyed by the effects of the sins committed after baptism. Through the sacraments of penance and anointing, we come into contact with Christ and his healing power. Just as Jesus raised the dead to life (Matt 9:18–26; Luke 7:11–17; John 11:1–44), so he infuses his divine life into our souls, which were dead after sin. It is, moreover, the same divine power that Jesus works in us through the sacrament of anointing, by which he both forgave the sins of the paralytic and caused his useless body to be fully restored (Matt 9:18). We will talk more specifically about the effects of these sacraments as we treat each one.

4. Do the sacraments heal beyond the individual?

The human person is by nature a social being. As social beings, human actions, for good or for ill, affect more than just the person who does them. While all my deeds are personal acts for which I alone am responsible, the effects of my actions, including my sins, reach beyond the realm of my personal being. Sin "injures human solidarity" (*CCC* 1849). A society, or any group of people, can only be as good as any of its members. Human actions that are contrary to the good of the individual diminish the person who engages in them and necessarily adversely affect the rest of society.

Christ did not come to save society; he came so that every person who receives him in love might be healed and transformed and so live by divine grace. To the extent that a person allows the divine life to permeate the entirety of his or her life is the extent to which society will also be transformed. The remedy for the ills of society begins with the healing power of the sacraments, which transforms the individuals who comprise it.

Nor must we forget that the church is a society, albeit a divine one. United to Christ, those who are living by the grace of the sacraments constitute the church. Thus, the public witness of the holiness of the church is greater to the extent that the transforming power of the sacraments is evident in each of her members.

Stressing the social aspect of sin in his 2007 document on the Eucharist, Pope Benedict XVI points to the relationship between the Eucharist and the sacrament of penance. He observes that sin is never a purely individual affair; rather, all sin damages the ecclesial communion of which our baptism has made us members. Penance not only heals the individual person of sin; it also affects the entire body of Christ, the church. When a penitent is absolved from serious sin, he or she is able to return to the Eucharist, effecting "the restoration of full ecclesial communion" (*SCar* 20). The priest's words of absolution make clear what has always been the case with this sacrament: that the penitent is reconciled with the church, the body of Christ, and, concomitantly, with God. A personal relationship with God can never be a private relationship; the relationship is always as a member of Christ's body, the church. To use the analogy of healing, think of the Christian who is wounded by sin as a sick member of the mystical body of Christ who causes weakness in the entire body. When that person is healed of the sickness of sin, the whole body is restored.

The sacrament of the anointing of the sick also has social ramifications. This sacrament unites the sick with Christ's self-offering for the salvation of the world, so that the sick, too, can participate in the redemption of the world within the mystery of the communion of saints (*SCar* 22). Thus, even the weakness that the Christian experiences as a result of serious illness, and death itself, is an opportunity for drawing personal grace, as well as grace for the strengthening of the church when they are suffered "with and in" Christ. When we consider that Christ died for the entire human race in order to make of us an offering to God and to make us his friends, we see the dignity and power of this sacrament that makes us, with our infirmities, participants in that great offering. We begin better to understand the meaning of St. Paul's words: "I am now rejoicing in my sufferings for your sake, and in my flesh I am completing what is lacking in Christ's afflictions for the sake of his body, that is, the church" (Col 1:24).

PART TWO

The Sacrament of Penance

A. Names of This Sacrament

5. Why do we call this sacrament "penance"?

Of the several names that this sacrament is called, "penance" is perhaps the quintessential title for both historical and theological reasons. It is the name that has been applied to this sacrament beginning with its practice in the early church. The word comes from the Latin *paenitentia* (literally, "penitence"), which refers to repentance or remorse for wrongdoing. Penance, or *poena* in Latin, is the punishment one undertakes in order to make amends for sins. This sacrament is aptly called penance because here the penitent, inspired by divine grace, approaches Christ through the confessor in order to change or convert from sin. Just as in human relationships we seek to make up for past failings by doing good for the person(s) we have hurt, so with God the sinner is moved to show regret by some act of atonement or penance. In the sacrament of penance, the act of conversion is consecrated to God (*CCC* 1423). Interior sorrow for sin is authentic and effective only when "it is translated into *deeds and acts of penance*" (*RP* 4; my emphasis).

It is important to remember, however, that this penance is meant to be medicinal, not penal. God is not interested in degrading us; he wants us to be healed of anything that has marred the divine image in us. Hence, penance is always undertaken with a view to being restored to full human flourishing so as to attain to the life of glory.

6. Would it be more proper to call this the "sacrament of reconciliation"?

The various names given to this sacrament each highlight an essential aspect of the sacrament. It is possible to refer to this sacrament by any of its typical names. It is called the sacrament of reconciliation because the chief purpose for which Christ gave us this sacrament is that we might be reconciled to God.

To reconcile means to bring two or more entities together again so that they are in agreement; so that they are harmonized. Thus, in the sacrament of reconciliation, we are set right with God after having sinned. But we are also set right with one another, that is, with the church. It should be noted that this reconciliation is not something we initiate; rather, it is the love of God, which reaches into our lives. God reconciles us to himself—with our cooperation, of course.

7. Isn't penance also called the "sacrament of conversion"?

It is helpful to consider the Greek word for conversion: *metánoia*, literally, allowing the spirit *to be overturned* in order to make it *turn toward* God (*RP* 26). It is a complete change of heart.

Conversion, signifying a change or a turning in attitude and behavior, is yet another aspect of the sacrament of penance. Penance, as the sacrament of conversion, actually makes Christ's call to conversion sacramentally present. It is the necessary first step in returning to the Father, from whom we have strayed (*CCC* 1423). Thus, our attention is drawn to the parable of the prodigal son, who, in the midst of his horrible plight, came to his senses and decided to *turn back* to his father (Luke 15:18). It is the type of conversion to which Jesus calls us when in Mark's Gospel he says: "The time is fulfilled, and the kingdom of God is at hand; repent, and believe in the gospel" (Mark 1:15, RSV). This requires that a person take stock of him- or herself with sincere honesty, first of all recognizing that he or she is a sinner. It is, as Pope John Paul II said, "the essential first step in returning to God" (*RP* 13).

8. Why is this sacrament also called "confession"?

"Confession" is probably the most common name for this sacrament; it simply refers to an indispensable part of the sacrament, namely, the act of confessing or revealing one's sins to the priest. In so doing, one is humbly admitting to God the actual deeds, thoughts, or omissions that have weakened or, in the case of mortal sin, broken our friendship with God. We should begin by asking the Holy Spirit to shed divine light into our minds so that we can see our sins more clearly. By acknowledging our sins, we take responsibility for them as offenses against God and neighbor. We can make the words of Psalm 32:3–5 (NAB) our own:

> As long as I kept silent, my bones wasted away;
>   I groaned all the day.
> For day and night your hand was heavy upon me;
>   my strength withered as in dry summer heat.
>
> Then I declared my sin to you;
>   my guilt I did not hide.
> I said, "I confess my faults to the LORD,"
>   and you took away the guilt of my sin.

An older meaning of confession is "acknowledgement and praise—of the holiness of God and of his mercy toward sinful man" (*CCC* 1424). This gives us an important spiritual insight into this sacrament of healing. Rather than avoiding this sacrament out of shame or embarrassment over our sins, we can approach the confessional with confidence and even praise, with the expectation that God wants us to be healed more than we ourselves desire it.

9. Can you explain the meaning of another title: the "sacrament of forgiveness"?

The sacrament has this name because God forgives or excuses or cancels the debt we owe him as a result of our sin. He takes away the burden of the consequences of our sins. Worth noting is the fact that God does not merely take something away; when he pardons, he also grants interior peace to the penitent, who is made pleasing in the sight of God by this sacrament. This title is also related to the title sacrament of conversion; for when, moved by God's grace, we turn *from* sin, we turn *toward* God. It is only in this posture that we are able to receive forgiveness. In other words, forgiveness is part and parcel of being in a right relationship with God, being in friendship with God. Divine forgiveness is always available in this sacrament, so that nothing need impede our friendship with God.

This title for the sacrament (see *CCC* 1424) brings to mind the words of the Lord's Prayer: "Forgive us our trespasses *as* we forgive those who trespass against us." It is impossible to expect forgiveness from God when we ourselves neglect or, worse, refuse to forgive the transgressions committed by others against us. If we desire to experience the healing forgiveness of God, we must be willing to be instruments of healing forgiveness in the hand of God for others. Christ's teaching is recorded in the gospel parable about the man who owed an astronomical amount of money to his king and pleaded for more time to repay him. Amazingly, the king simply wrote off (forgave) the debt. But when that same man whose debt had been completely erased met a fellow servant who owed him a mere fraction of that, the man mercilessly demanded full and immediate repayment and had his fellow servant thrown into prison for lack of ability to pay. Jesus ends the parable with words that should chill us to the bone: "So my heavenly Father will also do to every one of you, if you do not forgive your brother or sister from your heart" (Matt 18:35). In the Sermon on the Mount, Christ teaches that "if you forgive others their trespasses, your heavenly Father will also forgive you; but if you do not forgive others, neither will your Father forgive your trespasses" (Matt 6:14–15).

10. Why was this sacrament at one time called "second penance"?

This name dates from the earliest centuries of the church (*paenitentia secunda*). The "first" penance was the first conversion from sin, typically including a lengthy preparation, and culminating in the sacrament of baptism. As the sacrament of justification, baptism makes one a child of God and empowers him or her to offer Christian worship. Concomitantly baptism completely purges the soul of all sin: original sin, as well as all personal sins a person has committed, no matter their gravity. The baptized Christian was expected to remain a true friend of Christ, guarding against any breach of friendship. In the event of a serious turning away from Christ, a person was expected to undertake a rigorous penance, imposed by the bishop, which might last even a lifetime. The final act of reconciliation after such a grave fall included the penitent's reintegration into the church with absolution from the bishop. In the first centuries of Christianity, there were no options for a subsequent penance after the second. One understands, then, the seriousness with which our forebears regarded both sin and penance.

Some of the early fathers of the church, including Tertullian (ca. 155–ca. 220) and St. Jerome (ca. 342–420), had an intriguing name for the sacrament: they called it the plank of salvation or the *second plank after shipwreck*. The idea was that life is like crossing the ocean so as to arrive at the shores of heaven; shipwreck is that dreadful condition of being awash at sea after the disaster of losing one's boat as a result of the storms of sin. Penance is the metaphorical plank of wood to which the stranded soul clings in order to make it to the port of refuge at the end of life. St. Thomas Aquinas uses this analogy: For those who are crossing the sea, the first help is to be protected in a sound ship, and the second help is to cling to a plank if the ship is wrecked; so, too, in the sea of this life, the first help is to preserve our integrity, while the second help is to regain our integrity through penance if we should lose it through sin (*ST* IIIa, q. 84, a. 6). Thomas then explains that the "sound ship" and preservation of integrity refer to the sacraments of initiation (baptism, confirmation, and the Holy Eucharist) and the state of freedom from serious sin.

11. Does the Penitential Rite at Mass forgive sin in the same way as the sacrament of penance?

While both the Penitential Rite at Mass and the sacrament of penance involve an admission of personal sin, they are very different acts. In the first place, the Penitential Rite at Mass is not a sacrament separate from the Mass but a preparation for the holiest prayer that the church knows: the Eucharist. In fact, at certain Masses the Penitential Rite is omitted in lieu of other rites, such as the blessing of and sprinkling with holy water. The Penitential Rite is a prayer of humility and repentance, offered prior to entering into the mysteries celebrated in the Eucharist—the saving presence of Christ in the scriptures and the sacrament of his Body and Blood. Here one examines one's conscience and acknowledges, before God and the church, the need for purification and the grace to participate worthily in this supreme act of worship of God.

It is quite different, however, from the sacrament that absolves a person from sin, particularly mortal sin. While the priest at Mass asks God to forgive us our sins, this prayer does not grant absolution from serious sins. The person who is aware of having committed a mortal sin is obliged to make use of the sacrament of penance. Such a person should definitely attend Mass, although he or she may not receive Holy Communion unless sacramentally absolved from all grave sins. The importance of praying at Mass, even if one is not able to receive Communion, cannot be stressed enough. God will speak to every person who seeks him and will give graces that move him or her to deeper union with himself.

The Penitential Rite for someone in grave sin is an opportunity to ask God for forgiveness for one's sins, as well as for the grace to go to the sacrament of penance and reform one's life.

Likewise, individuals who have been baptized in non-Catholic churches and are seeking to become Catholics should not see the Penitential Rite as sufficient to receiving Communion. Even more so is this the case for persons who are not Catholic and have no intention of becoming Catholic. This helps to clarify the frequent misperception that the Penitential Rite prepares everyone, without exception, for Holy Communion, although St. Thomas Aquinas sees it as forgiving venial sin, as when he teaches that any act of charity done for love of God removes venial sin (*ST* IIIa, q. 87, a. 3).

B. The Sickness of Sin

12. What is sin?

Sin is "nothing else than a bad human act" (*ST* I–II, q. 71, a. 6). Here St. Thomas is not referring to poorly executed acts, as when a quarterback accidentally fumbles the football or a cook adds too much salt; rather, he means that the human person is created by God to know and love all that is good and, as a result, to act virtuously, knowingly, and willfully. Consequently, any human act (or inaction) that is opposed to true goodness is sinful. A human act is one that is done by a human being knowingly and willingly. In other words, an act done while sleepwalking is not a human act because the will is not properly engaged in the state of sleep. Furthermore, "true goodness" means that the human act does not merely *seem* good. For instance, when a person is hungry, it may seem good at the moment to eat an entire three-pound box of chocolates at one sitting, but clearly this is not at all an action that will promote good health; it is, therefore, a bad action even if it has the appearance, to some, of being good.

St. Thomas goes on to say that an act is evil when it does not measure up to the way God made things to be (otherwise known as the eternal law). There is, then, an external, objective standard by which one can determine whether one's actions are good or bad, be they matters of words, deeds, or even desires (*ST* I–II, q. 71, a. 6). But a sin is not merely a matter of breaching a cold legal structure: it is also an offense against God, whose plan it is for every human being to be happy and fulfilled by loving him first and then all other creatures in right order. The horror of sin, far from being some arbitrary breaking of a law, is that it breaks one's relationship with God (*CCC* 1850). One in fact says to God, at least implicitly: I don't care about my true happiness and flourishing; I will decide what's best for myself apart from you; I love myself more than I love you. No relationship can survive such self-centeredness—hence, the need for the Divine Physician whose forgiveness is necessary for healing what one's sin has destroyed.

13. What is mortal sin?

Mortal sin is another, and often more common, way of speaking about grave sin. We find in 1 John 5:16–17 a distinction concerning sins that are mortal, or deadly, and sins that are not. All wrongdoing is sin, St. John says, but not all sin is mortal.

The word *mortal* comes from the Latin word for death and refers to the serious effect of this sin, namely, spiritual death or the destruction of divine life, or grace, in the soul of the sinner. It is a turning away from God, a breach in our friendship with God, "by preferring an inferior good to him" (*CCC* 1855). We cannot lay claim to sanctifying grace or the life of charity because this kind of sin is directly opposed to love of God and neighbor. To use an example from human friendship, I cannot truthfully claim to be the friend of someone while at the same time committing some serious offense against that person. My wrongdoing results in the death of our friendship. And so it is with God, only more so because there is nothing a human being can do to make up for offending the almighty and transcendent God. The healing must come from God himself.

While we all sin, not all sin is mortal. There are three conditions for a sin to be considered mortal and all three must be met simultaneously. For a sin to be mortal, it must involve grave matter, be freely or deliberately consented to, and be done with full knowledge of what one is doing. If any one of them is lacking, the sin is called *venial*.

For example, if I, with full knowledge, willfully shoot and kill my innocent friend, I have committed a mortal sin. The grave matter here is the taking of an innocent life, while the knowledge and willfulness of the act show that I knew my action was wrong but did it anyway. I may not have considered at the moment of shooting that this would also rupture my friendship with God, but, nevertheless, I would have known that murder is contrary to the law of God.

Let's examine this example with a different twist. Suppose that I shot and killed my friend while we were hunting, but that it happened this way. During a hunting expedition with my friend, he tells me that he is going to the cabin to rest. Later, while tracking my prey, I see a rustling movement in the distance. Not seeing the bright orange vest meant to alert me to my friend's presence, and believing that he is resting in the cabin, I take aim and shoot, with the horrible result that I have killed him. I thought that I was setting my sights on my prey, not my friend. In this illustration, both full knowledge of the object of my bullet and my free consent of the will to kill my friend are lacking, even though the act obviously involves a most grave matter. The result is that, while I will experience a great deal of grief and remorse, no mortal sin has been committed.

On the other hand, pretending not to know what I am doing actually increases the free character of the act. We all know that it is not true ignorance by which I "accidentally" shoot my hunting partner with whom I have recently had a disagreement, claiming that I thought it was a deer in the bushes. Similarly, it is clearly stealing when I pretend to not recognize the bank teller's error in giving me one hundred dollars more than I am supposed to receive.

Some reduce mortal sin to "an explicit or formal contempt for God or neighbor" (*RP* 17) and thus mistakenly teach that it is impossible, or nearly impossible, for a person to commit a mortal sin. As this argument goes, if a person commits what some would call a serious sin, but does not specifically think of offending God, there is no mortal sin. This is quite wrong. Does a husband who is not thinking of his wife when he sleeps with another woman therefore fail to offend her by his adulterous action? The very act is an affront to a spouse because it is intrinsically disordered. It is possible, then, to change one's fundamental orientation away from God by even one serious sin freely committed.

For further study on serious sin see also Matthew 18:15–17; 1 Corinthians 5:1–5; 2 Corinthians 2:6–10; and Hebrews 6:4–6.

14. What is considered to be "grave matter"?

The essence of grave matter is found in the Ten Commandments (*CCC* 1858). It's not so much a question of asking if one of the commandments has been broken, but whether the sin committed is made up of the "stuff" of the Ten Commandments. The commandments are not meant as a list of things to do or not do, but are the instructions God gives for people to flourish as human beings. Seen in this light, then, the breaking of the commandments is understood for what it is: an affront to God, an opposition to the order God has established for individuals to be happy, and an offense against both oneself and one's neighbor. Notice that the commandments don't spell out the details of every possible instance of their abuse. They instruct about those things that are most important for a happy and fulfilled human existence. One might say that they deal with the essentials in life: giving God his due, and giving what is due to one's neighbor and one's self in terms of life, honor, ownership of goods, truth-telling, and sexual relations.

Some sins are worse than others. Taking an innocent life is certainly a graver sin than taking someone's goods. This is not to say, however, that stealing is less of a sin than murder. Rather, it points out the weightiness of the sins that have greater goods as their object.

Likewise, communicating falsehood is always a sin because truth-telling is essential to interaction among rational beings. Yet, there is a continuum of gravity by which one judges that lying about someone's reputation is quite different from a so-called white lie.

Moreover, judging the gravity of a sin involves considering who was harmed by the sin. For example, lying to one's spouse is graver than lying to an opinion pollster. Additionally, the state of life of the person committing the sin affects the gravity of the sin. For instance, while neglecting the obligation of Sunday Mass is a mortal sin for all, it would be graver in the case of a priest than for a layperson.

A word of caution about the content of the Ten Commandments: it would be foolhardy to think that only certain sins are covered by these ten divine laws. Rather, these laws apply broadly to the generic sins they address. For example, the commandments do not mention drunkenness or substance abuse. Yet, since these sins cause great harm, to one's own body at the very least, they might be considered under the heading of protecting human life, as covered by the fifth commandment: Thou shall not kill. You may wish to consult part three of the *Catechism of the Catholic Church*, which deals with morality in light of the Ten Commandments. What is to be avoided is the mentality that, since this or that sin is not really grave matter, or is less grave than something else, it's okay to commit it. God gives us the Ten Commandments so that we may be guided to all that is good; they also guide us to hate sin, that is, to hate what thwarts us from attaining all that is truly good and, indeed, robs us of what good has been given us. And, the ultimate good for each person is union with God in love.

It is helpful to learn about the seven capital sins, called this because they give rise to other sins or vices: pride, covetousness, envy, anger, gluttony, lust, and sloth. In addition, there are the traditional "sins that cry to heaven for vengeance": willful murder; sins against nature (such as unnatural sex); oppression of the poor (e.g., foreigners, servants, widows, and orphans); and injustice to the wage earner (*CCC* 1867).

I recommend two other scripture passages that are important for forming the conscience concerning grave matter: 1 Corinthians 6:9–10 and Galatians 5:19–21. Some may find the contents surprising!

15. What is venial sin?

Venial means excusable or pardonable. Venial sin refers to sins that weaken my relationship with God by offending him in some way, although not to the point of destroying the friendship God has initiated with me. To put it another way, an offense is venial when at least one of the qualifiers of a mortal sin (grave matter, full knowledge, or full consent of the will) is missing. Typically, it involves a matter that is not serious. If the matter is serious, but there was lack of full knowledge about what I was doing or I did not completely consent to the sin, then it is venial.

Some people think of venial sin as inconsequential because it does not involve a break in friendship with God. Surely, no one loses the prospect of eternal happiness in heaven or goes to hell for committing a venial sin. Nevertheless, venial sin is not without its consequences. No friendship, particularly divine friendship, goes undamaged even though the slights suffered may not be serious. The first effect of venial sin is that it weakens charity. Venial sin also indicates that a person is unduly attached to a good less than God. This results in the inability to make progress in the life of virtue and ultimately results in temporal punishment. When venial sins are committed deliberately and without repentance, a person is gradually disposed to commit mortal sin (*CCC* 1863).

In order to visualize the harm that venial sin causes, think of a blazing bonfire. The great fire signifies the burning love of the soul for God, fueled by divine grace. To remove just a branch or two will not greatly diminish the fire; however, repeatedly plucking sticks or removing logs from the fire will diminish it. If such behavior is left unchecked, one risks losing the fire altogether. St. Augustine suggests a different image. He says that while we live in this world as human beings, we cannot help but commit light sins. But he warns us not to take lightly such "light" sins: "If you take them for light when you weigh them," he cautions, "tremble when you count them. A number of light objects makes a great mass; a number of drops fills a river; a number of grains makes a heap. What then is our hope? Above all, confession..." (*In epistulam Johannis* 1, 6).

16. What are "sins of omission"?

Most of the time one considers sin as something one does, whether by thought, word, or action. It is also possible, however, to sin against God, neighbor, or self by *not* doing, by *failing* to think, speak, or act according to the norms of natural or divine law. What might be surprising is that sins of omission are not always merely venially sinful; they can be mortal sins as well. Thus, one will want to examine one's conscience concerning sins of omission prior to making a sacramental confession.

Several examples, not meant to be exhaustive, may help to clarify what is meant by "omission":

- not worshiping God as is his due, by thought, word,or deed
- not caring for the poor or for others in need of help
- not acting kindly toward others, such as with simple gestures or words
- not defending others when their true rights are being trampled
- not giving of one's time, talent, and treasure to Christ's church
- not living up to one's responsibilities in the family
- not speaking out on important social issues
- not exercising civic responsibilities
- not taking care of one's own health and fitness

- not being responsible for gifts received from God
- not protecting human life

This last example is worth further comment, living, as we do, in an age when human life is so often devalued. While this is not the place to discuss in detail the moral principles surrounding those who are gravely ill or dying, it is essential to understand that ordinary medical assistance and care are owed to all human beings. When one's action or even negligence causes the death of a person for the purpose of ending that person's suffering, one commits murder, which is at the same time both an affront to human dignity and a most grave offense against God who creates life (*CCC* 2277). Palliative care is essential for someone suffering great pain, but we may never confuse the effort to help someone in pain, or to end pain, with ending a human life.

17. What if I am not sure whether I have committed a mortal sin?

If, after careful examination of your conscience, you still have doubts about whether the conditions for a mortal sin are present, there are several things to keep in mind. First, try to calm any fears in your soul by remembering that God is merciful and wants to heal us. It is important not to fall into the trap of despair or over-anxiety, which only serves to keep us from turning trustingly to our loving God. Endless attempts to try to remember the details and motivations are usually done in vain because the memory cannot be forced in this way. Second, sincerely pray the Act of Contrition, resolving to avoid the sin in the future and to go to confession. Third, the doubt itself, provided that your conscience is conformed to God's law and the teachings of the church, would seem to indicate that culpability is diminished to some extent. Therefore, you may receive Holy Communion. Finally, make these matters known to the priest in confession and follow his counsel.

If you have sought the help of a regular confessor, he will be in a better position to give you the spiritual advice you need.

Related to this is the situation of a person who commits a sin that is objectively venial but who intended to commit a mortal sin. The confessor must take the intention seriously and treat the sin as a mortal sin, giving the appropriate counsel and penance.

18. What are the effects of sin?

Sin is to the human person what sickness or disease is to the physical body. It destroys the happiness and human flourishing that God intends for every person he has created. By choosing a grave evil (or mortal sin), or preferring a lesser good to God, one turns away from God, thereby severing one's relationship with him. In so doing, one gives up the gift of divine life, which is the grace of the indwelling presence of the Blessed Trinity. One forfeits, as well, the infused virtues of prudence, justice, temperance, and fortitude. In addition, the person who commits mortal sin is deprived of the seven gifts of the Holy Spirit: wisdom, understanding, counsel, fortitude, knowledge, piety, and fear of the Lord. The ultimate price for mortal sin is the loss of eternal happiness with God in heaven. There is only one alternative: eternal punishment in hell. Moreover, sin is also a revolt against oneself. This is because sin is a rebellion against God's order, a key component of which is the happiness of every human person. Thus, sin makes a person unhappy because it is ultimately self-destructive. As we have seen above, venial sin is also harmful. The person who desires a sound soul will avoid even venial sin just as a healthy person avoids contact with the flu virus.

Some people think of sin as "fun" and the faithful following of Christ as dull. The fact is that, while sin falsely promises pleasure or even apparent happiness, sinful pleasure is always fleeting and damaging because it makes one less a person, less whole, less human. It is like seeking to contract a life-threatening disease, thinking that it will be "fun." Nothing could be further from the truth regarding sin, which necessarily results in diminishment of the person and, therefore, in unhappiness. Only divine grace, by which we participate in the life of God and friendship with God, makes a person more fully human, healing the defects caused by sin and perfecting the soul. Seeking fulfillment in anything less than God leads only to frustration because nothing finite can satisfy the human desire for happiness. "You have made us for yourself, O God, and our hearts are restless till they rest in thee" (*Confessions of St. Augustine*, Bk 1).

19. Why is there punishment for sin?

Sin is its own punishment. In other words, since sin is the deliberate choosing of a lesser good over God, a limited or finite happiness instead of eternal happiness, one gets exactly what one wanted. When we think of the consequences of sin in these terms, we begin to see that God does not need to punish us; we do that to ourselves. Every choice we make has consequences. If a student chooses to play games rather than learn from the homework assigned by the teacher, the result will be ignorance. The teacher does not punish the student with a poor grade. Rather, the poor grade was the choice of the student, even if at the time he or she did not immediately and directly choose the low grade. Likewise, abusive language or actions used against a loved one harms the relationship. There can be no healthy relationship in such a case. By harming another, the abusive person also harms him- or herself. Thus, we can see that sin has its built-in punishment.

But there is more. Since every human being is made in the image and likeness of God, *by* God, every person, whether he or she realizes it or not, is a child of God. There is not one action any person can do apart from being a child of God. In committing a sin, even a nonbeliever is still acting as a child of God and offends God. The offense is more or less great to the extent that the sin is more or less damaging to oneself or to others. Thus, there is always another person being affected by every sin. It's never just a matter of a private sin, nor can it ever be just a matter of a sin between another person and myself. Always and everywhere and at all times, God is present and therefore God is being offended.

To speak of offending God does not mean that God's feelings are hurt. It is, rather, a matter of treating God *as* God. And since we are made for God, to be eternally happy with him, every time we sin (privately, with another, or against another), we necessarily damage our own potential for true and real happiness, the kind of happiness God intends for each person to experience. God is offended that we refuse the gift he offers: happiness resulting from his friendship.

No one would be so dull as to think that, in spite of hurting a friend, the friendship will flourish. It is all the more true of friendship with God. In addition to all the other consequences of bad acts, every sin, then, actually demeans the sinner; it makes a person less human. Therein is the punishment.

Sin has two consequences. First, if the sin is grave, the immediate consequence is the breaking of friendship with God. It is the choice by which one forfeits eternal life and merits eternal punishment (the privation of God, meaning hell). But the other consequence for every sin, including venial sins, is that I become attached in some disordered way to someone or something less than God. Any sin is self-demeaning and damaging to one's own dignity and worth as a human person.

We should never think of God as vindictive for inflicting punishment on us, any more than we would think of a friend as vindictive for being offended by abusive words. On the other hand, because God is infinite, only he can restore us to friendship with himself after grave sin. That is, only our participation in the passion, death, and resurrection of Christ Jesus, with heartfelt repentance, can write off the debt of eternal punishment. Even so, there remain the remnants of our sins, temporal punishments. Everyone who has ever hurt a loved one knows that even after a break in the friendship has been healed, there is always more to be repaired and restored. So it is with all repented venial and mortal sins. (See Q. 71.)

20. What is the "sin against the Holy Spirit"?

Jesus says, "Therefore I tell you, people will be forgiven for every sin and blasphemy, but blasphemy against the Spirit will not be forgiven. Whoever speaks a word against the Son of Man will be forgiven, but whoever speaks against the Holy Spirit will not be forgiven, either in this age or in the age to come" (Matt 12:31–32; also Mark 3:28–29, Luke 12:10).

On the surface, these words of Christ are puzzling. We know that our Lord desires to forgive all sin, even the sin of his crucifixion ("Father, forgive them; for they do not know what they are doing," Luke 23:34). Thus, it seems odd that the one sin that is unforgivable is the sin against the Holy Spirit.

Blasphemy against the Holy Spirit is contempt for God, exhibited in one's thoughts, words, or actions. In the passage above, taken from Matthew's Gospel, the Pharisees had just accused Jesus of using the power of the devil to expel demons from people. Time and again they refused to believe in the divinity of Jesus. The hardness of heart of the Pharisees, similar to the hardness of heart of the impenitent sinner, prevented them from seeing the action of the Holy Spirit at work in their midst.

There are two reasons this sin is unforgivable. First, it is not so much that God cannot forgive a sin against the Holy Spirit because of some limit to his mercy. It is, rather, that the person who sins against the Holy Spirit has hardened his or her heart against God. Such a person rejects the mercy of God, refusing even to acknowledge one's own sins. In other words, forgiveness is unobtainable because the sinner is not at all open to it. Just as one needs to have one's hands open in order to receive a gift, so the sinner must be open to the grace of forgiveness. Moreover, the more one persists in such a state, the harder becomes the heart, such that, at the end of life, one remains unrepentant, leading to the loss of eternal life (*CCC* 1864).

Second, the sin is unforgivable because it is a denial of God's power. It is possible to deny God's power by despairing of salvation (maintaining that God can never forgive this or that sin), or, on the contrary, to presume salvation by trusting in oneself rather than in God. The one who blasphemes against the Spirit shuts out the working of divine grace, with the risk of the loss of eternal life.

All Christians should pray to be protected from such sins and for the grace to be always docile to all the workings of the Holy Spirit.

C. Conversion and Penance: An Age-Old Remedy

21. Why does penance begin with conversion?

Whenever a person undertakes to do an act of penance, even outside the realm of divine worship, one is motivated by sorrow for having wronged another and endeavors to express that sorrow by some deed of atonement. Thus, when the driver of a car backs into the neighbor's motorcycle parked in the street, that driver will stop and turn around to both apologize and make restitution. The key to true penance is turning around, turning away, from the wrongdoing, and setting on the right course of action. When penance is done without conversion, there is no real change in a person and his or her acts of penance become empty show. So, the husband who secretly cheats on his wife while out of town may seek to assuage his guilt by bringing home a special gift, but if he has no intention of changing his behavior in the future, that is, turning away from the sin, then the penance (in this case, an act of devotion) is meaningless.

Doing penance means that we reestablish the balance and harmony broken by sin and that we change direction even though it may entail sacrifice. This is particularly evident in the parable of the prodigal son, Pope John Paul II says (*RP* 26). The wayward son, coming to his senses, turns away from his life of shame and decides to return to his father, planning out what he will say and do in repentance. It is the classic example of interior conversion (see Q. 7) and a return to the good, with the attitude of externally showing remorse with penitential acts. In the case of the prodigal son, the penance he plans to carry out is to work as a slave for his father.

To say "I'm sorry" is not just to mouth a few words; it is a matter of changing course, whether the matter be small or life-altering.

22. What does the Old Testament have to say about penance?

The Old Testament abounds with teaching and examples of communal and personal expiation for sin. Though the concept of *sacramental* penance is not found in the Old Testament, the theme of seeking forgiveness from God is prevalent. By God's command, the chosen people of the Old Testament participated in rituals and offered sacrifices to atone for their sins, but could never have the experience of being interiorly justified in the eyes of God by divine grace. This is because the grace of justification comes to us only through Christ. It was the perfect sacrifice of Jesus on the cross that struck at the root of the disease of sin. In the Christian dispensation, baptism begins the life of grace in us, and the sacrament of penance restores grace if we have lost it through sin. Conversely, Old Testament forgiveness was not an interior cleansing and healing of the soul. The best that could be hoped for was an external declaration that God would overlook their sins. It is the difference between putting a bandage on a cancer and actually removing the cancer and healing the wound.

Of all the Old Testament sin-offerings possible, the ritual that became Yom Kippur stands out as the most important. Also known as the Day of Atonement, Yom Kippur, in Judaism, is the annual day of fasting, prayer, and quiet, as commanded by God in order to atone for sins. As prescribed in Leviticus 23:15–32, the high priest offered animal sacrifices in order to expiate his sins and the sins of the people. It was the one day of the year he was permitted to enter the holy of holies in the temple to invoke mercy and healing for transgressions of the Law. Afterward, the high priest laid his hands on the head of a living goat and *confessed* all the sins of the people. This *scapegoat* was then driven off to the desert, symbolically carrying off the transgressions of the people (see Lev 16:20–22). Although the synagogue service (worship conducted apart from the official Jewish temple) precludes animal sacrifices, the Jewish people, even today, make a public confession of sins in unison.

It is important to recognize, however, that it is always God who initiates purification and justification. It is God who gave his people the gift of Yom Kippur for the forgiveness and healing of their iniquities. Atonement (literally: *at-one-ment*, or "to be one with") is the necessary human response to the divine initiative. Christ is the flawless atonement and satisfaction for the debt of our sins, the Lamb of God who takes away the sins of the world (John 1:29).

23. Does the New Testament contain evidence for the sacrament of penance?

Yes, it certainly does. First, when the Lord Jesus began his public ministry he preached the necessity for repentance and a life of reform if one was to be his follower and belong to the kingdom of God (Matt 4:17; Mark 1:14–15). But Christ also came to forgive sins in order that we might have his life in us, lest anyone think that the life of conversion and reform is merely a matter of human effort. John the Baptist said of Jesus: "Behold, the Lamb of God, who takes away the sin of the world" (John 1:29, RSV). Jesus' life culminated in the greatest act of love, forgiveness, and healing the world will ever know: his death on the cross. The very words he uttered as his hands and feet were being nailed express the meaning of his crucifixion and are intended for each one of us: "Father, forgive them; for they know not what they do" (Luke 23:34, RSV). His life and death were for the expiation of our sins (cf. Heb 2:17). "He himself bore our sins in his body on the cross, so that, free from sins, we might live for righteousness; by his wounds you have been healed" (1 Pet 2:24).

Second, Christ gave his apostles and the church the authority to forgive sins. The first instance of the conferral of this power is found in the account of Peter's profession of faith that Jesus is the Son of God. Jesus tells Peter that Peter himself is the rock upon which Christ's church is built. He then entrusts to Peter the power to bind and loose, to permit and forbid (Matt 16:13–19; 18:18; cf. Isa 22:22). The words *bind and loose* mean that if you exclude someone from your communion, that person will also be excluded from communion with God; and those whom you receive back into your communion will also be welcomed back by God into his. Reconciliation with the church and reconciliation with God are inseparable from each other (*CCC* 1445; see also 2 Cor 2:5–11).

Another clear instance of Christ giving the apostles the divine power to forgive sins is found at the end of John's Gospel (20:21–23). It was the evening of Resurrection Sunday and the apostles had locked themselves in the Upper Room in fear. Jesus appeared in their midst and greeted them with words of peace. He told them: "'As the Father has sent me, so I send you.' When he had said this, he breathed on them, and said to them, 'Receive the Holy Spirit. If you forgive the sins of any, they are forgiven; if you retain the sins of any, they are retained.'"

Third, the power to forgive sins did not end with the death of the apostles. Christ willed that this ministry continue in every succeeding generation. Before he ascended into heaven, Jesus said that "repentance and forgiveness of sins is to be proclaimed in his name to all nations" (Luke 24:47). Reconciliation always begins with God's initiative, but God has willed that all grace, including that of the forgiveness of sins, be mediated through the church that he established. This is clear from the preceding gospel passage of Christ giving power to the apostles (see also 2 Cor 5:18). If seeking forgiveness from God were only a matter of the sinner asking forgiveness from God in the privacy of his or her heart, Christ need not have given the power to forgive sin to his disciples.

Having received the power from Christ to forgive sins, the apostles in turn handed on that authority to their successors (bishops and priests). Just as the power given to the apostles to baptize and preach was something to be handed on as a permanent gift to the church, so too was the power to bind and loose. Thus, this great gift of being freed from sins has been passed down through every age. The very same power that Christ gave to Peter and the apostles is the power a priest exercises today when he absolves a penitent from sins.

24. What evidence do we have of Christians making use of penance in the centuries after the time of the New Testament?

Surely the primitive church appreciated the possibility of penance for sins committed after baptism. While grave sin was not expected among the baptized, nevertheless, the first Christians would have recalled the words of Christ to Peter and the apostles by which he gave them power to bind and loose sin.

We do possess ancient documentation that portrays penance as part of the life of the early church. For example, the *Didache*, sometimes called in English *Instructions of the Apostles*, is a text, dating probably to the first century AD, that teaches Christians about the moral life and ecclesiastical practices. Specifically, it says: "In the church you shall acknowledge your transgressions, and you shall not come near for your prayer with an evil conscience. This is the way of life" (4:14). It also enjoins Christians to gather every Lord's day to break bread and give thanksgiving, after having confessed their sins, in order that their sacrifice may be pure (14:1).

Sources from the first and second centuries also show the necessity of penance, even if they do not reveal much of the liturgical procedure. One finds examples in Clement of Rome's *Epistle to the Corinthians* (ca. AD 95–98), the letters of Ignatius of Antioch (ca. AD 110), *The Epistle of Barnabas* (ca. AD 130–40), and others. A work called *The Second Epistle Ascribed to Clement of Rome* (ca. AD 150–60) urges repentance for sins committed after baptism while there is still time, because once the soul has departed the world, the individual can no longer confess sins nor do penance. Another second-century work considered authoritative by Christians of that time, *The Shepherd of Hermas*, makes specific reference to the possibility of reconciliation after serious sin, but apparently only once in a lifetime.

Additionally, we find early references to the power to forgive sins. In the so-called *Canons*, attributed to bishop and martyr Hippolytus (ca. AD 170– 236), the prayer for the consecration of a bishop asks that God grant him "the spirit of clemency and the power to forgive sins" (c. xvii). The *Apostolic Tradition* of Hippolytus has this prayer: "Grant him, O Lord almighty, through your Christ, the participation of your Holy Spirit, in order that he may have the power to remit sins according to your precept and command, and to loosen every bond, whatsoever it be, according to the power which you have granted to the Apostles" (chap. 3).

25. Did the church during the early centuries have a specific ritual for the sacrament of penance?

While first- and second-century Christian documents such as the *Didache*, the *Second Epistle of Clement*, and *The Shepherd of Hermas* witness to the idea that sins could be forgiven after penance, the details of a rite for reconciliation used by the Christians of the early centuries remain unknown to us.

The external rite of penance has changed through the centuries, but the internal substance of the sacrament has not. After a serious fall from grace, Christians from the earliest times sought reconciliation through their local pastor, the bishop. Well aware that not only was God offended by sin, but that the church as a community was harmed and in need of healing, the church originally emphasized the communal over the private aspect of penance. In other words, while one who sinned would confess the actual sins privately to the bishop (or, in other cases, a delegated priest), he or she was then enrolled in the *order of penitents*, a special category for Christians who had sinned seriously after baptism. As a member of the order of penitents, one publicly undertook rigorous forms of penance, including fasting, prayer, and works of charity, for an extended period of time. It was not uncommon for these forms of penance to last for years with the intention of bringing about true interior conversion from sin. Typically, such reconciliation was a once-in-a-lifetime experience. Christians realized that a second serious fall from grace carried dire consequences for their salvation. Then again, one would expect that, after a lengthy period of public penance, interior conversion would be deep and lasting. Finally, once the public penance was completed, the bishop prayed over the penitent, granting communion with the church. Often this happened on Holy Thursday, making it possible for the reconciled penitents to experience anew the joy of Christ's resurrection, having realized his power in their lives over their past sins.

What should be obvious in the description above is the communitarian and ecclesial nature of the sacrament of penance. While the particular revelation of one's sins to the bishop may have been done in private, the enjoined acts of penance and reconciliation were anything but. This is not to be confused with totally private confession (including the private assignment of penance and its completion), which did not evolve until centuries later. Earlier, the Christian community may not have known what sins a person committed, but it knew who belonged to the order of penitents. This underscores the teaching that to be reconciled with God meant that one had concomitantly to be reconciled with the Christian community. This is because Christ gave the power of binding and loosing to the church. It was only in the early Middle Ages that the communal aspect of penance receded.

Because of the rigor of the penance and unrepeatability of the sacrament, people began to put off the sacrament until their deathbeds, clearly a dangerous proposition for any soul seriously wounded by sin.

D. The Priest as the Minister of Penance

26. Why is it necessary to confess to a priest rather than to ask God in my heart for forgiveness?

Actually, this question can be misleading because it is necessary both to beg forgiveness interiorly *and* to confess mortal sins to a priest. Simply going to confession without any interior contrition, as we have seen above, is worthless. On the other hand, interior contrition must be expressed exteriorly as well.

There are various reasons people might highlight for confessing to a priest. Some stress the psychological benefit. Others emphasize the social dimension of confession, namely, the healing that comes from seeking pardon through the priest who represents the entire church against whom we have sinned. Still others point to the Bible for evidence that confession is what God instructs Christians to do in order to be forgiven and healed. The fact is that all these statements are true.

On the evening of the day on which he rose from the dead, Jesus appeared to the apostles who were hiding in the Upper Room. The gospel states that Jesus breathed on them and said: "Receive the Holy Spirit. If you forgive the sins of any, they are forgiven them; if you retain the sins of any, they are retained" (John 20:22–23; cf. Matt 9:8). Although God alone can forgive sins, Christ has delegated to the apostles his divine authority to absolve. Christ desires that the healing of the wounds of sin be available to all the world. He does this through the church when the men who are ordained have conferred on them Christ's own divine power to bring the fruit of his passion and death to each soul in need of forgiveness.

Notice the pattern that Christ follows in giving us this sacrament (and all sacraments, for that matter). God could simply have declared, at some moment in history, that all sin for all people was forgiven, and that from that moment on, the world would have a fresh beginning. But he didn't do that. He went through the trouble to become a human being, to live among us in the flesh, to suffer and die and be buried, and then to rise from the dead and ascend to heaven. He did this because God respects the way he created the world to be. We humans are not only spiritual beings; we are physical beings as well. We have a body and a soul. In his plan to rescue us from the dominion of sin and death, Christ did not make an immaterial declaration for our souls only. He saved us precisely through his body. In other words, he uses what is material in order to heal and sanctify both the material and immaterial.

Furthermore, Jesus continues to heal and sanctify us, not because we somehow reach back into the historical scripture and try to claim the effect as our own in the present moment. Nor do we somehow simply make an act of faith, hoping that God will forgive. No, God lives and works through the ministers who are now his agents of grace, just as the apostles were made agents of grace. Christ empowered them, as we see in John 20:22–23, and they, in turn, have passed on to others the power given them by Christ. This passing on of authority is important. Without it, the power of forgiving sin would have died with the last apostle. But it makes no sense to say that Christ gave the apostles the power to forgive sins for the people of only that time, leaving all subsequent ages suffering from the very sickness Christ came to heal. Hence, the Christian community, from its earliest days, has understood that the ministry the apostles received from Jesus was passed to their successors, the bishops, as well to the bishops' collaborators, the priests. (See 2 Cor 5:18; *CCC* 1461.)

Christ instituted this sacrament in order that we could experience the power of his passion, death, and resurrection in the present moment. We have the divine promise that when we approach him through his priests, we will receive the forgiveness of our sins. He wants it that way for our good and so that we need have no doubt about the effect.

This ties in with the psychological benefit of confessing to a priest. While it is always humbling to have to admit to another person that we have done something wrong, the reassurance of forgiveness that the other expresses is more than worth the humiliation because we know that what was wrong has been made right. Imagine the situation of never knowing with certainty whether one has been forgiven because of the inability to face the person wronged. One may pretend, presume, or hope that forgiveness has been given, but one will never be certain. All too often is this the case when someone dies before a loved one could ask forgiveness. For Christians, Christ allows himself to be sought through the priest who shares in the very priesthood of Christ, making it possible for us to receive his forgiveness even two thousand years after his ascension into heaven.

Last, our reconciliation and sanctification come from Christ through his priests, but, as with all grace, through Christ's body, the church. When Christ gave his apostles the authority to forgive sins, he gave it because he had made them members of himself. They were not merely associates of Jesus or simply his followers. He gave them an entirely new life such that they became branches grafted onto the vine stem of Christ Jesus (John 15:1–8). It is only by being attached to Christ that anyone can claim to have his life and bear fruit. St. Paul uses the analogy of the body in 1 Corinthians 12 to teach us that all ministries and gifts in the church come only to those who are members of the body, content to exercise their proper function. No one can take it upon him- or herself to forgive sins apart from the power that comes through the church. The *Catechism* makes this clear when it teaches that the bishop, as the visible head of the church, is the one who is principally entrusted with the ministry of reconciliation (*CCC* 1462). When a priest absolves sins, he does so only by the authority given him by the church. It is because he represents Christ that he also represents the entire body of Christ, and when he pronounces the words of absolution, he is restoring the repentant sinner to the Christian community, the church. The priest is the agent of Christ and of the church, binding the wounds of sin and restoring the branch to the vine where it may be nourished with Christ's life and love.

27. In an emergency, if no priest is available, may we confess our sins to someone who is not a priest?

There was once a practice of "lay confession" but it is no longer in use. In the early centuries of the church certain nonordained monks or nuns acted as spiritual advisors, often giving advice on various penances to be undertaken for particular sins. However, sins considered to be grave still needed to be submitted to the bishop, who would assign the penance and later give absolution. Instances of lay confession can be found even in the late Middle Ages. Interestingly, St. Thomas Aquinas (among other medieval theologians) believed that there was a salutary effect to lay confession when a priest was unavailable. He taught that a deathbed confession to a layperson in the absence of a priest is *sacramental*; however, it is not a *sacrament* because of the lack of the priestly absolution. Moreover, if the dying person survived, the penitent would be obliged to seek sacramental absolution (*Scriptum Super Sententiis* IV, q. 3, a. 3.2). Aquinas envisioned special graces of spiritual healing at the moment of death, presuming, of course, that the penitent did not put off calling a priest in due time.

The disappearance of lay confession can be attributed to the development of the theology of the sacraments, as well as to abuses of the practice. In response to Martin Luther's denial that a priest had any power more than a layperson to absolve sins, the Council of Trent defined that confession to a layperson has no sacramental power.

While the number of priests in some cities may be few, I am rather hesitant to recommend lay confession because of the confusion in the minds of some regarding the proper minister of the sacraments of healing. When one becomes aware that one is dying, it's time to see a priest. Modern communication and transportation make it possible for a priest to be summoned and to arrive in order for a person to prepare for death. The one exception might be when Catholics are living in remote mission regions, where the celebration of the sacraments is rare or even nonexistent.

Not to be confused with lay confession is the commendable, and perhaps at times even essential, practice of asking forgiveness of those who have been hurt by one's sins during life. It is important, obviously, to seek pardon as soon as possible after offending someone, but when this has not been done, one has a duty to make amends on one's deathbed, if it is at all possible. In some cases this will also entail forgiving those who have wronged us, sometimes in very serious ways.

28. Is it true that the priest in the confessional is considered to be both judge and dispenser of mercy?

Some would prefer to think of the priest only as the dispenser of mercy, and the scriptures themselves might seem to justify such thinking. Jesus tells us that he has come to seek out and save those who are lost (Luke 19:10). Time and again he makes it clear that his mission is one of mercy. Reflect on the parable of the shepherd in search of only one lost sheep out of a flock of one hundred. He goes into the wilderness to search for it and, finding it, lays it on his shoulders and carries it home (Luke 15:4–7). Or again, ponder the parable of the prodigal son, who has squandered his entire inheritance. His father stands outside the house scanning the horizon for any sign of his possible return and then welcomes him home with great festivity (Luke 15:11–24). Christ does not condemn; it is the one who rejects God's love who condemns, possibly unto eternity, himself or herself. We glimpse the unhappiness of one who rejects the extravagance of God's love in the person of the brother of the prodigal son, who refuses to join the feast given at the return of his brother (Luke 15:25–32).

However, God is not solely all-merciful, doling out forgiveness; nor is he solely all-just, meting out punishment. He is perfectly both at the same time. Perhaps the clearest image given us in the scriptures of Christ as the merciful judge is the moment of his crucifixion. While one of the two criminals crucified with Jesus blasphemes him, the other confesses his guilt and asks Jesus to remember him when Jesus comes into his kingdom. Christ replies: "Truly I tell you, today you will be with me in Paradise" (Luke 23:43). Christ does not deny the sin; he pays the price for it.

In the sacrament of confession, the sinner, by placing himself or herself before the priest, comes before Christ, the same crucified Christ who delivered the criminal into paradise and who rose from the dead in order to give us paradise. The sinner comes to Jesus, the just and merciful judge, begging pardon and mercy. In acknowledging one's sins at this judgment seat, the sinner is freed from eternal punishment at the judgment at the end of life (*CCC* 1470). In fact, it is the medicine of confession that prevents the experience of sin from degenerating into despair (*RP* 31).

So, it is the case that every instance of merciful forgiveness and welcome is necessarily preceded by the recognition, or judgment, that something or someone was lost. There can be no real grant of mercy without such a judgment. It is in this sense, then, that one must think of the priest as judge. As a doctor must judge the extent of a disease, so the priest exercises judgment in order to heal with this "medicinal sacrament" (*RP* 31).

In hearing confessions, the priest "is at once both judge *and healer*...constituted by God as a minister of both divine justice and divine mercy," both for the glory of God and the good of souls (*CIC* 978, emphasis my own). The priest does not sit as some imperious official listening to the penitent's confession. Rather, his role is one of service, acting *in persona Christi*, in the person of Christ, whenever he is celebrating any of the sacraments. The priest-confessor is called to unite himself to the intention and charity of Christ and prayerfully to entrust the penitent to the Lord's mercy (*CCC* 1466). Pope John Paul II insisted that the confessor have the "human qualities of prudence, discretion, discernment, and a firmness tempered by gentleness and kindness," as well as a deep spiritual life. He must himself practice the life of penance

(*RP* 29). This is why, incidentally, a priest prays before hearing confessions; he wants to be prepared, to have the mind and heart of Christ as an instrument of divine justice and mercy, to know how to speak to each soul what that one needs to hear.

29. How does a priest know which penance to assign?

As we noted above in the section on the history of this sacrament, penances during the early centuries were typically public and rather onerous, such as observing long periods of prayer and fasting, doing works of charity, making a pilgrimage to a holy site, and so forth. The strict once-in-a-lifetime opportunity to receive the sacrament of penance was relaxed when Celtic monks from Ireland, such as St. Columban, began traveling as missionaries to the Continent, already in need of reform, in the sixth and seventh centuries. St. Columban is credited with introducing to Europe the possibility of frequent (as opposed to once only) and private confession. Based on a system of tariffs, he also developed a classification for assigning penances for various kinds of sins. These lists, called "penitentials," began to circulate, although complete uniformity regarding the sacrament was lacking. Priests, especially those with less training, welcomed the penitentials as a convenient help in dealing with moral situations and assigning penances. In the Middle Ages, the penitentials were replaced with books that detailed the rites for sacramental penance and with theological works that helped the priest understand and apply the principles of moral theology. In later centuries, the attitude of confessors tended to overemphasize the priest's role as judge, as the sacrament was seen more in legal terms than as a help for the penitent to grow in virtue.

In the post–Vatican II period, some people joke that no matter what sin a person commits, even murder, the priest will absolve him or her and simply assign the penance, "Say three Hail Marys." While modern-day penances are a far cry from those imposed during the early church period, priests must still consider several things. First and foremost, he must receive the best theological training, one that integrates all the components of moral and systematic theology. Though I may be accused of partiality for insisting that every seminarian be grounded in the virtue theory of fellow Dominican St. Thomas Aquinas, I also know any number of non-Dominican theologians who would agree. But theological training does not and cannot end with graduation from the seminary. Ongoing study of moral theology is imperative because the priest will always encounter new souls with unique problems who desire the healing of the sacrament and knowledge about virtue in order to be truly free.

Second, the priest must take into account the penitent's state of life, that is, single, married, in religious vows, or a deacon, priest, or bishop. One's state of life may make a sin more or less grievous. Then, in light of the sins confessed, the priest wants to give the best penance for the penitent's spiritual growth. The confessor will consider such factors as the type of sin and its gravity, and the penitent's age and ability to complete the penance. The priest must keep in mind that the satisfaction, or completion of the penance, is meant to help the penitent restore the order disturbed by his or her sins and to supply an appropriate *remedy* so that he or she may be cured of the sickness suffered (*PCS* 6c). The priest will avoid the extreme of being overly strict or severe in his role as judge, as well as the converse of being too lax in seeking to be merciful.

Each time he sits down to hear a confession, the priest will want to ask the Holy Spirit to enlighten his mind and give him the insights he needs to deal well with each soul. With the Holy Spirit's help, the priest will know whether this or that penitent would benefit best from offering prayers, doing works of charity, undertaking acts of self-denial, or some other sacrificial activity. Sins of theft, property damage, damage to someone's reputation, and the like, require that restitution be made. Sins involving grave public scandal may necessitate that the penitent make a public declaration of repentance.

Finally, the penance must be something that the penitent can actually accomplish. In other words, it must not be impossible, for not even God commands the impossible. It should not, therefore, be something beyond the penitent's ability, nor should it be perpetually ongoing. I once went to confession to a priest who gave me the penance of never sinning again. Truly, I desire never to sin, but the only person who could truly not commit even a venial sin was the Blessed Virgin Mary. We all commit venial sins daily. So the penance was impossible. This does not discount the fact that more serious sins and crimes may require more weighty penances, as one might imagine in the case of cold-blooded murder.

30. Are there priests who are not able to hear confessions?

While every priest has, by the fact of being ordained, the power given by Christ to absolve sins, not every man who is a priest has the authority to do so. He must also be given the faculty—a license, as it were—to absolve sins. The local bishop of the diocese in which the priest resides grants this faculty to a priest judged to be competent, and puts it in writing because it is the bishop who has responsibility for the entire flock of the diocese entrusted to him. In a certain sense, the priest is the bishop's helper; he shares in the work of the bishop and needs to be officially delegated to carry out whatever duties are entrusted to him by the bishop. Thus, a priest needs faculties from the bishop so that proper order can be maintained in the exercise of this sacrament, particularly in the case of discipline of priests. One might think of the instance of a priest who, for one reason or another, has been removed from active ministry, whether for a short time or permanently. Likewise, a bishop may deem that a priest is unfit, perhaps temporarily, to hear confessions. When a person is in danger of death, however, any priest, including a priest who has been laicized (one who is allowed to live as a layperson), may absolve the penitent, even if a priest with faculties is present (*CIC* 976). This is because the church is concerned for the spiritual welfare of each person and thus gives the widest possible latitude in the dying person's choice of confessors, even though death may not be imminent. Finally, it should be noted that if a priest is in good standing in his diocese, he may hear confessions anywhere in the world, although another bishop may proscribe a particular priest from hearing confessions in that bishop's diocese.

E. The Rite of Penance

31. How does one prepare for confession?

Given that the sacrament of penance is a gift from God by which he heals our sins, he moves us by a special grace to seek out the sacrament. We are free, of course, to accept or reject that grace. The best way to respond to this grace is first to ask the Holy Spirit to enlighten our minds so that we know our sins and are sorry for them, with the intention to confess them. The next step is to make an examination of conscience, which means that we consider specific sins, whether of commission or omission. It is not sufficient simply to think about general areas in need of improvement or only about the most predominant sin. Rather, we should make this review humbly and truthfully. The examination is not a time for making excuses for ourselves. The best practice is to make an examination of conscience daily, for example, in a time of prayer just before going to bed. This way we become familiar with tendencies toward particular sins and will be able to bring this to our next confession.

It is recommended that the beginner have a guide when examining one's conscience, though even very "experienced" penitents sometimes find guides useful as well. Such a guide may help us recall sins that may have been forgotten. It may also help in forming the conscience: making sure that our conscience is properly formed and making us aware of instances where there has been a compromise in the moral life that may otherwise have been overlooked. For example, an inadequate catechesis may leave a person in ignorance about the obligation to worship God every Sunday at Mass. A good guide for the examination of conscience will cover a wide spectrum of behavior. Remember, the purpose of being aware of sin is not to increase the feeling of guilt but to bring to light those areas in need of healing by the Divine Physician. A good form of the examination of conscience from the official *Rites* is appended at the end of this book. Other well-prepared forms of the examination are available in some of the books listed in "For Further Reading."

32. What takes place during the sacrament of reconciliation?

Fundamentally, the rite of the sacrament of penance is composed of two elements: a penitent brings his or her sins to Christ for healing, and a priest, who stands in the person of Christ and the church, grants absolution, which gives special healing graces to the penitent. Both are essential for the integrity and validity of the sacrament. One without the other is not the sacrament, just as there can be no surgery, and therefore no healing, if either the patient or the doctor is missing.

That being said, this simple explanation carries with it certain presuppositions about both the penitent and the priest. First, it is a special grace of the Holy Spirit that moves the penitent to seek Christ's healing in this sacrament. This seeking of forgiveness has three aspects: contrition, confession, and satisfaction.

The very act of bringing to confession sins in need of divine forgiveness means that we are contrite, that is, sorry for having committed all the sins of which we are aware. Confession involves the disclosing of our sins to the priest. Satisfaction means that we seek to make amends for sins committed; it minimally involves a penance imposed by the priest and typically is completed after the absolution. More on each of these follows next.

33. What is contrition, and what is the "Act of Contrition"?

Contrition, essential to the sacrament of penance and the penitent's first act, means that we are sorry for and detest the sins we have committed, and we resolve not to sin again (*CCC* 1451). It is helpful to know that the word *contrition* derives from the Latin meaning "to grind, to crush." The knowledge of guilt crushes the soul, as it were. It is the sorrow we all experience after hurting someone we love. This is the essence of true or perfect contrition: sorrow motivated by love of the person(s) we've offended. Imperfect contrition is called "attrition" and refers to sorrow for sins from some motive other than love, such as fear of punishment or of retribution, or even chagrin to discover one's faults. It is important to know, however, that one may be sincerely sorry for one's sins but not *feel* sorry. True sorrow is an act of the will. Our feelings do not always coincide with our decisions. For instance, even in the midst of some difficulty in a family relationship that may cause a person to feel angry, there is an abiding love that transcends the feeling of anger. The decision to love a family member who is acting badly will move me to help the other out of love, in spite of my feelings. So it is with sorrow. We may be puzzled that we don't feel the emotion of sorrow sometimes, especially in confession. However, true sorrow is shown in the very act of deciding to turn from the sin, confess it, and avoid it in the future, that is, willing the means to the end, taking the steps necessary to avoid this sin in the future. We can be sure that God sees into the depths of the human heart.

We endeavor to come to the sacrament of penance with true contrition. But in the absence of the ability to know whether one has contrition or just attrition (imperfect contrition), the sacrament itself supplies whatever may be lacking in our contrition. In other words, I must bring at least attrition for my sins to the sacrament. The sacramental grace of penance completes attrition so that I may have divine forgiveness for all my sins. Spiritual authors make the point that the greater the sorrow for sin, the greater the increase of sanctifying grace in the soul. This leads to the greater overcoming of sin and the deepening of charity in a person's life.

Part and parcel of sorrow for sin is the intention to not sin again. This is called the "firm purpose of amendment." In fact, if this purpose of amendment is lacking, even if the priest should impart absolution, the sacrament is invalid. It would be like a spouse asking forgiveness for an act of adultery, knowing full well that he or she has no resolve to avoid the sin. Even if the other were tricked into forgiving the adulterer, the forgiveness would fall on a heart impervious to the gift. The firm purpose of amendment is not an absolute guarantee against all possible sin in the future; except for the Blessed Virgin Mary, we all commit venial sins. It is, however, a resolve to take all the steps necessary to avoid sin, including avoiding temptation and seeking to grow in virtue.

All of this is summed up in the prayer called the Act of Contrition, which every Catholic ought to memorize. The priest-confessor will ask you to make an Act of Contrition just before he imparts absolution. There are several versions of the prayer. I recommend this one:

> My God,
> I am sorry for my sins with all my heart.
> In choosing to do wrong
> and failing to do good,
> I have sinned against you
> whom I should love above all things.
> I firmly intend, with your help,
> to do penance,
> to sin no more,
> and to avoid whatever leads me to sin.
> Our Savior Jesus Christ
> suffered and died for us.
> In his name, my God, have mercy. Amen.

This, or any Act of Contrition, is not restricted to the sacrament or even to just this prayer. To grow in holiness and the virtue of penance, it is important to have the spirit of contrition through each day. This is built up by making repeated, even simple, acts of contrition when we sin, even venially, for example, "Lord Jesus Christ, Son of the living God, have mercy on me, a sinner."

34. What is involved in the actual confession of sins?

As we noted in question 8, Psalm 32 expresses the relief that confession of sin brings. Confession is the admission of having sinned in particular ways. In other words, one admits to having done, thought, or said something that disrupts one's relationship with God and the church, or to *not* having done or said something that ought to have been done. Sins, not faults or imperfections, are the matter for the sacrament. By "matter" is meant the actual sins that will be absolved by the priest. The confession of sins should be humble, direct, and integral, meaning "complete," in that we confess all sins, especially mortal sins, since our last confession. In other words, it is marked by simplicity, openness, and straightforwardness—not making excuses, not blaming others for one's sins, not telling the sins of others. Sins of a sexual nature should be confessed specifically as to the act involved, but simply and without details. If mortal sins have been committed since the last confession, they are all confessed first, according to kind and number. Circumstances that change the nature of the sin should also be confessed. For example, while attempted murder of any person is a sin, the nature of the sin is changed were someone to attempt to take the life of the pope, for example, or the life of an expectant mother. After mortal sins have been confessed, then venial sins are confessed. Confession is very much like showing wounds to the doctor in order to have them healed. It would make no sense to hide some hurt or ailment, or to pretend they do not exist or are inconsequential, and yet expect to be fully restored to health.

Confessing sins according to kind and number means that one names the sin and how many times it happened. For instance, someone might confess deliberately missing Mass on Sunday six times, fighting with one's spouse on two occasions, failing to forgive a coworker on one occasion, and secretly harboring covetous thoughts. Some people are mistakenly under the impression that one needs only to confess one area of life that is troubling the penitent. The difficulty with this is that things that trouble us are not necessarily sins. More importantly, by focusing only on one area of life, we fail to make an integral, or complete, confession, that is, naming all the sins we can remember since the last confession. We tell the number of times because each instance of the same sin is a separate offense, just as multiple cuts on the body each need to be treated although they are all the same type of wound. It also gives the priest an indication of the type of help or counsel he must give to help the penitent overcome the various types of sins.

It would be harmful to knowingly withhold one sin or another from confession, even if it causes great shame. St. Thomas Aquinas teaches that the shame that accompanies the confession of sins is itself remedial by reducing the temporal punishment we would have to suffer in purgatory (*ST* Supp., q. 10, a. 2). We can think of shame as a kind of sanitizing agent. The sting it causes is temporary but it purifies us so that we can enjoy full health, union with the Trinity. Thus, truthfulness is another important mark of a good confession. To deliberately mislead or lie to the priest is to abuse the sacrament (a sacrilege) and thus involves yet another serious sin.

35. Why is it necessary to confess the number of times a mortal sin has been committed?

There is no such thing as generic love or generic sin. Just as each act of love builds up a relationship, so each sin destroys friendship with God. Even the same act done repeatedly either makes a good act more meritorious or an evil act more grievous. Murder is horrible beyond description when even one human life is taken, but several murders committed by the same person constitute an unspeakable malevolence. One lie about another person is very bad because it damages a person's reputation, but repeating the lie to several others, or telling other lies about the same person, is more wicked. Moreover, when someone has hurt any one of us in several ways, we know that true reconciliation can happen only if each instance of wrongdoing has been adequately dealt with. A generic apology simply is not effective because each act of wrongdoing is a separate instance of knowingly and willfully acting against the true good of loving God. For this reason, we must take responsibility for each of those acts when we repent, just as we would when asking forgiveness from another human being. Owning up to our sins allows divine grace to penetrate even more deeply into the soul, healing the bad effects of each sin. Even if it is humbling to have to admit in confession the number of times a sin has been repeated, the healing will be even greater. Thus, it is always best simply and directly to confess the particular sins committed and how many times for each. When it is impossible to recall the exact number, say, because of a faulty memory or having been away from confession for a number of years, a general reckoning of the number suffices.

36. Is it necessary to confess to a priest in person?

Yes, in order for the sacrament of penance to be valid, the penitent must be personally present and receive absolution in that setting. We call this auricular confession (from the Latin *auricula* for "ear") because it involves the speaking of one's sins "into the ear" of the priest. It should be noted that the emphasis is on the proximate physical presence of the penitent and priest. Modern electronic communication devices such as telephones, video-phones, computers, faxes, and the like, obviously do not suffice to make two people physically present to each other. However, the hearing- or speech-impaired may use other means of communication in the sacrament, presuming, of course, that the penitent is in the immediate presence of the priest.

Someone might object that if a person has committed a grave sin and needs to be absolved, but is not able to reach a priest because of some dire reason (for example, distance or urgency), then the seriousness of the situation should override the rule about auricular confession. In these and similar cases, the penitent is advised to make a perfect Act of Contrition (see Q. 33) with the intention of going to confession as soon as possible.

There are several reasons why a confession must be auricular and not virtual. The first is the consideration of the sacredness of this liturgical and sacramental rite. It is sacred because we are approaching God. It would be irreverent and dangerous to trivialize the sacred, particularly a sacred reality that God himself instituted for our salvation.

Second, the more serious an act is, the more it demands personal presence. This is especially evident in the incarnation. God chose not merely to communicate his love and friendship at a distance, but entered into our world as a human being with all that that entails. Thus, all the sacraments require our physical presence.

Third, a serious disruption in friendship demands a personal expression of sorrow. Even on the level of purely human relationships, a mending of a broken friendship calls for the two parties to be in each other's presence. It is even more the case that, when we have offended God with serious sin, we would want to appear before him in person, as it were. This is what we do when we approach the priest in the sacrament of penance.

Two examples from scripture might help to illustrate the point. It is helpful to recall that Moses was told to remove his sandals when God appeared to him in the burning bush (see Exod 3:4–6). Similarly, the sacred rite of penance calls us to realize that we are in an unworthy state and yet we stand "in person" on holy ground in this sacrament. The second example is the prodigal son, who was in a faraway country when the horror of his actions became apparent to him. He got up and returned literally to his father. So, too, must we get up and return to our heavenly Father (see Luke 15:20). Anything less would be unfitting.

The sacrament of penance is a meeting between the repentant sinner and Christ through the mediation of a priest. Christ instituted all the sacraments, including penance, so that we might have a person-to-person encounter with him. When we consider that every sin is a personal offense against God and that it disrupts our friendship with God (see *RP* Introduction), it becomes clear that reconciliation also requires a personal response with all our being.

A fourth reason why a person must confess in person is that any other means of communicating one's sins or the priest's counsel does not guarantee the secrecy of the confession and would most likely constitute a breach of the seal of confession (see Q. 49). Even if the penitent were not concerned about others learning of his or her sins, the priest must take every precaution to maintain the seal of the confession.

37. How do I know if my confession was integral, meaning "complete"?

A confession is called integral, meaning "complete," when we have confessed all known sins since our last confession. In so doing, we must take care to ensure that we name the exact kind of sin and the number of times it was committed. Depending on the matter, more or less explanation may be necessary so that the priest-confessor knows what it is that he is absolving. For instance, it would be insufficient to simply state that one has sinned against the sixth commandment ("You shall not commit adultery"), or to say that one has sinned against chastity. In such a case, the penitent needs to specify what kind of unchaste sin was committed and how many times. Or, for instance, if one of the sins is theft, the penitent will need to explain what or how much was stolen from whom (not giving the name, but the type of person robbed). In this case, one might say: "I took $30 from the bank," or "I stole clothing from the department store," or "I robbed the collection from a blind man who was begging for money." Or again, if the sin involved the immoderate use of alcohol, the penitent would confess to being drunk on how many occasions.

If the penitent is vague, the priest may need to ask clarifying questions, but he will never ask for details beyond the kind of sin committed. For example, the priest may never ask the penitent the name of an "accomplice." Nor will he ever ask unnecessary questions, particularly in dealing with delicate matters.

Making a complete confession is important because it affects the validity of the sacrament. In other words, deliberately leaving out a mortal sin can make the sacrament void. It is yet another sin to lie about our sins or to withhold important information about our sins.

While making a complete confession is essential for the validity of the sacrament, the penitent should avoid the opposite extreme of giving too much information. The priest does not need to know, nor does he want to know, all the gory details of every sin committed.

38. What if I forget to confess a sin?

When preparing for the sacrament of penance, one must have the intention of making a complete confession, but it may happen that one forgets to confess a mortal sin. This does not apply to venial sins, since they can be forgiven in other ways. If a person remembers a serious sin after having gone to confession, it is simply a matter of bringing that sin to one's next confession. It may be the case, of course, that one never again recalls the sin, so this applies only when the memory of it arises. Once again, the medical analogy helps us understand why the confession of a forgotten sin is necessary. I would want to make sure to tell the doctor about some serious medical ailment on my next visit so that I can have the full benefit of being healed. So it is with sin. Sacramentally, we speak of submitting our sins to the "power of the keys," referring to the power given to priests to loose and to bind. The penitent wants to be completely unfettered of every sin. Grace effects a spiritual healing where once we were bound by guilt.

39. What is "satisfaction," and what is the purpose of making satisfaction?

Satisfaction is the completion of the penance, to make amends for sins. To refuse to complete the penance given in confession, whether outwardly or even interiorly, invalidates the sacrament.

The purpose of making satisfaction is a matter of justice. We see this in human relationships when one has wronged another. It is not enough simply to ask pardon of someone we have hurt. It is necessary to do something to make up for the hurt we caused. The greater the hurt, the more we are obliged to do something about it. For instance, the child who breaks a neighbor's window must not only ask forgiveness of the neighbor, but must also pay for its replacement. Stolen goods must be returned or paid for. The spouse who uttered harsh words knows that a simple "I'm sorry" is not enough; only a greater display of tenderness will act as a salve for this wound.

We refer to any wrongdoing as sin because the wrongdoing is also an offense against God. No one escapes the disintegrating effects of sin. The sinner and his or her relationships with another, the community, and God are all affected by sin, even "small" sins. All require healing. I think the example of overeating helps to illustrate the point. If I give in to my craving for chocolate to the point that I eat a half-dozen brownies in one sitting, I will show for my "sin" with a weight gain. I may wake up the next morning and tell myself I won't do this again, and even forgive myself for having given in, yet again, to my weakness for chocolate. But all the forgiveness in the world won't take away my excess weight. I will have to make up for the extra calories by increasing my exercise. The exercise is like the satisfaction or penance of the sacrament. I must do my part to atone for my sins.

Absolution removes sin, but it does not remedy all the disorders caused by sin. After being forgiven, the sinner still needs to recover full spiritual health by doing something more to make amends for the sin (see *CCC* 1459). While no one can ever fully make up for even the least sin that offends God, this fact does not negate the need to at least try to make amends as a matter of justice and charity. Thus, in carrying out the penance, the penitent allows divine grace to transform him or her into a person who is capable of greater love of God and neighbor. To blithely pretend that making amends does not matter begs the question of true conversion of heart.

40. What if I do not understand or remember the assigned penance?

Since satisfaction is a necessary part of the sacrament, we will want to make sure that we are able to carry out the penance. At times, making satisfaction will include some act of reparation in addition to the penance, such as making restitution for stealing or for sullying a person's good name. If we do not understand the penance that the priest gives, we should immediately and humbly make this known to the priest. Asking for an explanation needs to be immediate so that the priest can explain the penance or give a different one. We do this humbly, which is to say that it takes humility to admit that we do not understand what is to be undertaken or that some particular prayer is unfamiliar to us. It should be noted, as well, that if the penance is something we are incapable of doing, we should explain why this is the case so that the priest can help us to make satisfaction in some other way.

Should we forget altogether what penance was assigned, we can simply return to the priest right away and explain the situation (assuming that the priest is not occupied with a number of other penitents). Otherwise, we should simply try to recall a penance given in a previous confession and substitute that for the present moment. Furthermore, we should mention this substitution in the next regular confession, thus making sure, in the case of weightier matters, that the penance was appropriate. In the meantime, the penitent may receive Holy Communion at Mass.

In the unfortunate circumstance that the priest-confessor does not give a penance, intentionally or otherwise, we should rest assured that the sacramental absolution is valid since we were not refusing the penance. The priest has the responsibility, as part of the proper celebration of the sacrament, to impose a penance, even if only a light one. Otherwise, it is a disservice to the penitent, who has both a right to the proper celebration of the sacraments as well as a right to be treated with dignity, that is, to be recognized as capable of holiness and as one who desires to make satisfaction for past sins. In these cases, I recommend that the penitent offer at least some form of prayer in lieu of the assigned penance. I also recommend that the penitent, without being argumentative, demanding, demeaning, or preachy gently insist on receiving a penance from the priest.

41. When should the assigned penance be done?

Satisfaction is to be made, that is, the penance completed, as soon as possible after having received the sacrament. Not only does this ward against the possibility of forgetting to do the penance, but the desire to do penance can also be a sign of heartfelt sorrow for having sinned and a sign of heartfelt love of God. The possibility of neglect is always to be avoided.

Some penances may require a longer time to complete, as might be the case, for example, when one is asked to make restitution or to do something out of charity for another, or some other penance. In such a case, one may receive Holy Communion prior to the completion of the penance.

42. What is "absolution"?

Absolution is based on a Latin word meaning "to release from." It is the church that grants absolution through the priests who share in Christ's power to forgive sins and release sinners from the guilt of their sins. Thus, the sinner's friendship with God is reconstituted and the sinner reconciled with the entire body of Christ, the church, on whose behalf the priest acts. In the case of serious sin, eternal punishment is remitted through the sacrament.

It is worth reflecting on the words of the prayer that the church uses to reconcile sinners. With his hand extended over the penitent, the priest prays:

> God, the Father of mercies,
> through the death and resurrection of his Son
> has reconciled the world to himself
> and sent the Holy Spirit among us for the forgiveness
> of sins;
> through the ministry of the church
> may God give you pardon and peace,
> and I absolve you from your sins
> in the name of the Father and of the Son and of the
> Holy Spirit.

At the words invoking the blessed Trinity, the priest makes the Sign of the Cross over the penitent. The penitent makes a devout Sign of the Cross and responds, "Amen."

The prayer of absolution sums up God's work of re-creation and healing. Our merciful Father, like the father of the prodigal son in Luke 15, draws us to himself and heals the effects of our sins through the passion of Jesus Christ. This work of reconciliation is carried on, after the ascension of Christ to the right hand of the Father, through the Holy Spirit, whom our Lord has sent to us that we might have his life in us. The Holy Spirit is present in the mystical body of Christ, the church. It is always Christ, through his body, that gives sacramental graces. Thus, it is through the church as the body of Christ that we are forgiven our sins. When we are pardoned, we experience interior peace because we know that we are once again made whole; any fear resulting from our separation from God as an effect of our sins is taken away. The priest grants absolution in the names of the three Persons of the Trinity, for it is God who takes away the guilt of our sins through the ministry of priests, who are servants of the healing grace that God gives through Christ's body, the church.

43. Are there occasions when absolution is not granted?

No priest will ever delight in refusing absolution. I can say from experience that it is one of the most painful things for a priest to do. The confessor will always try to help the penitent to realize the seriousness of this situation and to rectify it by guiding the penitent to a proper attitude so as to be able to grant absolution. It should be noted that it has been a long-standing practice for confessors to take for granted that a person who approaches the sacrament of penance is being led by God's grace to be reconciled.

While a properly disposed priest will always want to absolve the sins he hears in confession, there are instances when he is unable to do so. There are several reasons why this might happen. First, if the sin is among those with an attached penalty that can be remitted only by the Holy See, the priest may defer absolution. For a fuller explanation of this, see later in this answer, in Q. 54, and in Q. 67.

Second, it may be the case that the penitent has not presented sufficient matter, namely, sins, for the sacrament. The purpose of the sacrament is to heal sin. If no sin is confessed, then there is nothing on which the sacrament can work, so to speak. In other words, if the penitent simply approaches the priest in the confessional to discuss some issue in his or her life, but there is no particular sin involved, then the priest does not give absolution, though he may choose to give a simple blessing.

Third, if the penitent is not properly disposed, it may not be possible for the priest to give absolution. There could be several causes for this, such as a lack of true sorrow for the sins committed, the unwillingness to amend one's life, the outright intention to commit those sins again, or the refusal to do penance or make satisfaction as directed by the priest.

Probably the most vexing situations for the priest arise when he is unable to grant absolution because of cohabitation and other marital sins. In order to be reconciled to Christ and the church in the sacrament of penance, persons living in trial marriages and free marriages (cohabitation) must first choose to reform these relationships. Likewise, Catholics who have sought marriage outside the sacrament will take steps to reform their lives prior to seeking the sacrament of penance in order to receive the grace of absolution. The most difficult situation involves the person who had a sacramental marriage but divorced and then remarried another person. The first marriage must first be annulled by a church tribunal before one is able to seek marriage again. Thus, the person in this case may not be absolved until this has been rectified. I direct the reader to Pope John Paul II's *Familiaris consortio* ("On the Role of the Christian Family in the Modern World"), 84, for a very clear teaching on this matter.

44. What is the prayer that some priests pray immediately after the absolution?

Once absolution has been granted by the priest, and the penitent has responded "amen," the priest says: "Give thanks to the Lord, for he is good." To this the penitent responds: "His mercy endures forever." At this point, the rite of penance gives the priest the option of ending the sacrament with several forms of the dismissal. Typically, one hears these words: "The Lord has freed you from your sins. Go in peace." Another option is an older prayer that was once more generally used for the dismissal: "May the Passion of our Lord Jesus Christ, the intercession of the Blessed Virgin Mary and of all the saints, whatever good you do and suffering you endure, heal your sins, help you to grow in holiness, and reward you with eternal life. Go in peace."

Though not essential to the rite of penance, priests are highly recommended to offer this theologically rich prayer. The text of the prayer helps the penitent to recognize that while the sacrament has a finite end in time, the penitent is called to continued conversion of life because conversion ceases only when perfection has been attained with the beatific vision. Thus, with this special blessing of the priest, the repentant sinner is able to offer not only the satisfaction imposed in that particular sacramental act but every moment of one's daily life as a means for growing in holiness. The help of the Blessed Virgin and all the saints through all ages, as well as all those daily (and even the smallest) personal acts of charity and daily personal crosses (again, even the smallest), may all be suffused with the power of Christ's passion to transform the penitent into a holy person. The ill effects of past sins are healed, making him or her more free to live a flourishing life. Thus, sin is vanquished and the sinner is led by Christ, day by day, to the banquet of eternal life.

45. Must the sacrament of penance always take place in the confessional?

It is not wrong, when a just reason exists, to hear confessions elsewhere than in a confessional (*CIC* 964.3). Such reasons might include "illness, deafness, claustrophobia, urgency, the desire to go to a particular confessor when a confessional is not available," and so forth. For instance, often enough people will come to the parish rectory (or, in my case, the Dominican priory) at times when the sacrament is not scheduled to be celebrated. On these occasions, one uses a room where there is sufficient privacy. I have heard confessions in airports (far away from the earshot of any passersby) and other places where the Holy Spirit is moving some soul to repentance and conversion. While I would prefer a more sublime setting for this sacrament, pastoral concern for the grace of the moment prevails.

That being said, there are several reasons why it is preferable to celebrate this sacrament in the confessional. The first has to do with the fact that the church is not merely a building; it is the dwelling place of God and a house of prayer (cf. Matt 21:13); when we are in it, we are standing on holy ground (cf. Exod 3:5). Considering that the sacraments are privileged encounters with Christ, what better place to do it than the house of God? Second, confessionals are constructed to ensure privacy for the penitent and the protection of the sacramental seal. Third, the physical church is also a symbol of the universal church with whom we are reconciled through the sacrament of penance. It is fitting, therefore, that we physically enter the place that represents both our return to the body of Christ and the healing that takes place in penance. Fourth, the confessional gives the penitent the opportunity to confess anonymously or, conversely, to have a face-to-face meeting with the priest.

This last point needs clarification. Canon law stipulates that confessionals, including "reconciliation rooms," are to be fitted with a fixed grille or screen between the penitent and the priest (*CIC* 964.2). A kneeler and chair must be provided for the penitent so that the penitent is always afforded the possibility of remaining anonymous. No one is ever bound to reveal his or her identity. This allows the penitent the greatest freedom to make a sincere confession without having to be concerned about the added burden of embarrassment or scandal. Moreover, the priest himself may feel more comfortable, in this particular forum, hearing confessions behind the screen.

F. The Effects of Penance

46. What happens to us after we receive the sacrament of penance?

Christ gave us the sacraments so that we might share in the communion of life with God that was broken by sin. Penance is the sacrament whereby the effects of sin are healed by grace. Our relationship with God that has been ruptured by sin is restored, and we are freed from the burden of guilt so that we can live freely as children of God, growing in intimacy with the Blessed Trinity. We can speak of God's desire to see each one of us live in complete human freedom. Consider a healing that Christ worked in a synagogue on a Sabbath day. Eyeing a woman in the synagogue who was possessed by a spirit that drained her strength for eighteen years, and who was so badly stooped that she could not stand up straight, Jesus called out to her, telling her that she was healed, and immediately she was able to stand erect (Luke 13:10–13).

Yet, freedom is meant, not for making up and changing the rules as we please, but for making or doing something beautiful. As one of my Dominican brothers puts it, true freedom is freedom for excellence, not the freedom of indifference. It is the difference between writing gibberish (simply because one can!) and writing words that communicate meaning. Living more perfectly means greater personal flourishing, which in turn leads to happiness.

Penance, then, makes possible ongoing conversion, for we all are prone to sin. The sacrament brings the mortal sinner back to life and offers all sinners the grace to experience deeper devotion through discipline. Just as the athlete must discipline his or her body in order to perform well, so it is with the Christian's body and soul.

An important aspect of penance when we have committed mortal sin and have expressed our full contrition is that the grace of the sacraments we have previously received, such as baptism, confirmation, orders, and marriage, revives in us. If we have committed mortal sin, we have been deprived of sanctifying grace and the grace of the sacraments we received in the past. Thus, for example, the grace of marriage is not available to someone in the state of mortal sin until that person is sincerely contrite. The bond of marriage remains, even if the grace does not. When we are absolved of serious sin in confession, the graces of the sacraments we have previously received revive. Similarly, both the merits we had previously received from God, and the gifts of the Holy Spirit (the virtues and fruits) are restored. These help to sustain the moral life in us (cf. *CCC* 1830).

47. Why do we need to be reconciled to the church when we have sinned?

As St. Paul teaches in 1 Corinthians 12, we are members of one body. If one member suffers, the entire body suffers, and if one member is honored, so it is for the whole body. Sin, we have seen, not only disrupts a person's relationship with God, it also affects the church. To cut oneself off from God is necessarily to cut oneself off from Christ and his body.

Conversely, it is impossible to be reconciled to God without also reconciling with the church. Besides worshiping God through Christ, the church preoccupies herself with the work of reconciliation entrusted to her by Christ (cf. Matt 16:19; 18:18; 28:16–20).

This is all the more wondrous when one thinks about the possibility of being forgiven by God through a perfect Act of Contrition after mortal sin, that is, contrition motivated by love of God. If one is forgiven, why is such a person required to go to confession before returning to Holy Communion? None of us is an island, as shown by St. Paul in his teaching on the body of Christ. To return to Holy Communion is to return not just to a private relationship with Christ but to communion with Christ's body. Thus, I must seek to make right with the entire body what wrong I have done, even private or secret sins. This was, after all, the basis for public penance in the early church. Notice, too, the words of absolution that communicate the reality that God has given the ministry of reconciliation to the church: "Through the ministry of the church may God give you pardon and peace." "*Reconciliation with the church is inseparable from reconciliation with God*" (*CCC* 1445, emphasis in the original).

48. Why does a person sometimes experience guilt even after going to confession?

The experience of guilt is the awareness or feeling of personal responsibility for having committed wrongdoing of some sort. In the context of our discussion, it refers particularly to the alienation we cause in our relationship with God as a result of sin. Thus, guilt alerts us that something is amiss with regard to the objective moral truth and that we need to turn back to God in repentance and reparation. Once we have repented of our sin, guilt has served its purpose. We might call this true or "good" guilt. Romano Guardini, a renowned theologian, wrote in *The Living God* that, in coming to terms with the guilt of our sin, we must first realize that wrong has been done to God, and that "wrong has been done to the gentle and holy life that He has awakened in the heart, to the holy trust that binds Him to His child." Our guilt makes us aware that we deserve to be punished, but the answer is not to cover over the guilt and reassure ourselves that our intentions were good. Rather, we are urged by truth to say: "Give these things their full weight. Then I will come to you. I am God." The human heart is great, says Msgr. Guardini, but "God is still greater…greater than all this wrong."

However, the remnants of guilt may remain after we repent and go to confession, or worse, we may continue to feel shame to the point of self-loathing, falling prey to demonic suggestions that God wants nothing to do with us. Nothing could be further from the truth. This kind of guilt is false and is born of fear, usually the fear of not being forgiven by God.

It's important to recognize this difference. Moral relativism, which is the basis for denying any objective norms of good or evil, also refuses to admit that guilt can be good. Yet, guilt is good precisely in that it moves us to respond to the evil actions or inactions we have perpetrated; guilt moves us to come to terms with our sin, that is, to atone for it. This kind of guilt informs us that we need to confess our guilt and repair the damage caused to others, including God. It awakens in us the need for the sacrament of penance.

The ultimate healing for guilt comes from the grace of sacramental penance. Having been reconciled with God and having made reparation to our neighbor for our sins, we might say that guilt has done its job and it should dissipate.

When false guilt rears its ugly head, we should calmly turn to God in our hearts in a spirit of repentance, recall his mercy and forgiveness, and praise him for his forgiveness. It is important to keep our focus on God and not on ourselves. Continuing in a spirit of repentance does not mean to dredge up the memories of absolved sins, but rather to allow grace-induced sorrow to serve as a way of telling God that we love him and to allow his mercy to transform our souls.

Dostoevsky's Father Zosima, in *The Brothers Karamazov*, gives the most excellent advice to those who experience false guilt. A widow has come to him. Her dead husband had made life unbearable and used to beat her severely. The reader never learns what her sin was because she whispers it in Father Zosima's ear. She then tells him that though it has been three years since her crime, she has become ill thinking of her past deed in spite of the fact that she had been absolved in confession. Father Zosima is both consoling and encouraging, telling her never to be afraid of anything. His wisdom shines through, however, when he instructs the woman never to relax the spirit of repentance, for God can forgive everything. Sin truly repented of is always forgiven by God, for nothing can exhaust God's boundless love. The key, he insists, is to "repent without ceasing," confident that God loves you even with your sin.

It is in knowing God's tender mercy that we can show mercy to others, overlooking and excusing their sins against us. God intends that his gift of divine charity should overflow from our lives into the lives of all around us, healing divisions of every stripe.

G. The Secrecy of Confession

49. May a priest ever tell someone what he has heard in the sacrament of penance?

Among the obligations a priest holds most sacred is the promise to keep secret the sins he has heard confessed. This is referred to as the "sacramental seal." In other words, whatever the priest learns in confession is "sealed." There are no exceptions whatsoever to this rule. Whether the sins confessed are mortal or only venial, every priest is obliged to maintain the strictest secrecy in order to protect the penitent. Even should the priest not be able to grant absolution, he is still bound by the seal to not reveal anything from the confession. Or, as I vividly recall my professor telling me in the seminary: "You may not even bat an eyelash when it comes to the possibility of betraying a penitent." So seriously do priests take the seal that they will not even say whether they have heard an individual's confession.

A priest may not use to the detriment of penitents the knowledge he gains about their lives in the sacrament of penance (*CCC* 1467). If, for example, one of my students confesses to me that he has cheated on an exam I just gave, I may not use that knowledge when correcting his exam or assigning his grade. Praying privately for the penitent, however, is not detrimental to him or her, and is advisable.

A fascinating and excellent portrayal of the sacramental seal is found in Alfred Hitchcock's *I Confess*. This 1953 film is about a priest who hears the confession of a thief and murderer. Circumstantial evidence, including insinuations made by the murderer, points to the priest as the murderer. He can say absolutely nothing to defend himself when tried for the crime. I won't give away the ending of this movie; you really must see it for yourself.

The reason for the seal is that, in this sacrament, the penitent discloses the secrets of his or her conscience. No one has access to another person's conscience except God himself. God, and God alone, deservedly knows the secrets of the soul. Thus, the priest stands in a most privileged place when a person reveals his or her sins. Ordained by Christ to forgive sins, the priest must act as Christ does, not only in the matter of granting divine forgiveness, but also imitating the secrecy that God himself keeps regarding all our sins.

50. Is the priest allowed to speak with the penitent about the confession at some later time?

It is never permissible to break the seal of confession. Therefore, the priest should never bring up a past confession with a penitent. On the other hand, it may happen that a penitent, subsequent to the confession, wishes to discuss some aspect of the confession. I have had the experience a number of times, for example, of a penitent desirous of maturing in the life of the Spirit who asks for more advice or help in overcoming this or that sin. This happens frequently in ongoing spiritual direction. The other occasion for continuing a discussion that began under the seal is when the penitent is unknown to the confessor, such as would be the case when the confession was done anonymously. It is practically impossible for the priest to know which penitent confessed which sin(s). At any rate, when a person approaches me after having gone to confession and asks to discuss some matter that surfaced during that time, I simply remind the penitent that I am under the seal of secrecy and that it is necessary for him or her to mention the matter anew outside the confessional. This leaves the penitent free to continue the conversation or not and protects the inviolability of the seal of confession. The priest may never presume to know which penitent confessed which sins. The best advice, which all priests know from their training, is to say absolutely nothing to anyone at anytime about anything that happened during confession.

51. Isn't it burdensome for the priest to know and keep secret the sins of others?

Actually, no. There are several reasons for this. First, a well-trained priest knows that, after offering Mass and preaching the gospel, the most important work in his ministry is the administration of the sacraments of healing. Through a life of ever-deepening prayer, the priest perceives that, whatever else he does, he belongs first in the sanctuary, in the confessional, or at the bedside of the sick and dying. It is his joy, then, to carry out this responsibility entrusted to him by Christ to bring divine grace to others.

Second (since grace perfects nature), the priest, by virtue of his ordination, receives the grace of office to carry out all the work that belongs to his life. He must, of course, be open to that grace. This openness happens when he spends time with Christ in daily prayer. With regard to the sacrament of penance, he receives the grace to love sinners; indeed, to seek them out. Just as Christ did not come for the healthy but for the sick, so the priest is to look for those sheep who are lost, who are wounded by sin or caught in the thickets of worldliness. No soul is beyond saving, because it is Christ, through the ministrations of the priest, who saves. With the grace of office comes the grace to deal patiently with sinners, to pray for them, to offer them life-changing counsel. There is also the grace to look beyond the sins confessed and see the soul for whom Christ died. Priests pray, too, for the "grace of forgetfulness," that is, the grace to never remember anyone's sin(s).

Third, the priest knows that the burden is not his in the first place; it is Christ's. It is the burden of the cross, on which Christ suffered for sinners victoriously. If we may speak of any burden at all, it is the "burden" of being completely conformed to Christ, including the daily offering of the sacrifice of Calvary at the altar, for the conversion of sinners and for the return of the repentant to share in the fruits of Christ's sacrifice. Only a man foolish enough to think that the salvation of the world is on his shoulders would be unduly burdened. Fortunately for the priest, God is in control and the victory over sin has been won.

Fourth, there is also the joy of knowing that someone has been reconciled with God and given the grace of having his or her sins healed, so that this son or daughter may flourish in the Father's kingdom. In the parable of the prodigal son (Luke 15), just before our Lord teaches about God's desire for his wayward children to return home, he says, not once but twice, that there is more joy in heaven over just one repentant sinner "than over ninety-nine righteous persons who need no repentance" (Luke 15:7). The priest is to be like the father of the prodigal son; he is out looking for the lost in order to restore them to their rightful dignity. With the angels, he, too, rejoices to impart the grace of absolution. Forgiveness, not the wallowing in the misery of sins committed, is the end of the sacrament of penance.

Last, the priest knows that we are all sinners. In fact, the best priest to approach in the confessional is the one who is most aware of his own sinfulness and his own need of God's mercy; he will be zealous in dispensing God's mercy freely. He will also want to assist the penitent by offering, even secretly, his own additional penance as a priest in order to help the penitent to be healed of the remains of sin.

52. What if a person overhears someone else's confession?

I recall one elderly person who was hard of hearing and shouted his sins to the priest in the confessional. To anyone nearby, it was impossible not to hear one or another part of his confession. Thus, it may happen that you inadvertently overhear someone else's confession. One may never eavesdrop, of course.

Whoever hears any part of what happens in the confession of another is bound by the same secrecy that pertains to the priest. It is best to alert the priest that you overheard one part or another of the confession. It will help him know that he needs to take precautions against others hearing confessional matters in the future. He will also remind you of your own obligation to secrecy.

It should be noted here that when an interpreter is used in this sacrament (for example, a sign-language interpreter helping a deaf person), the interpreter is also bound by the seal.

53. May a priest break the seal of confession if the state requires it?

Even if the state were to require it, no priest may reveal what he has learned under the seal of confession, even the smallest venial sin or the least detail, including the identity of the penitent. No civil or ecclesiastical institution, no subpoena, no threat of punishment (including death) can compel the violation of the seal.

There have been martyrs for the seal of confession. I highly recommend viewing Alfred Hitchcock's *I Confess* (see Q. 49) for an excellent portrayal concerning the fate of a priest framed for murder by the murderer himself, whose confession the priest has heard. While there is no factual evidence for it, a legend grew up that King Wenceslaus IV of Bohemia (*not* "good King Wenceslaus" from the hymn, who was Wenceslaus I) had St. John Nepomucene killed in the fourteenth century for refusing to reveal the content of the queen's confession. More definite are these examples: In 1620 in Moravia, because he refused to break the confessional seal, St. John Sarkander was tortured on the rack, branded, and burned, only to suffer yet another month before he finally died in prison. Fr. Andreas Faulhaber, a parish priest, was hanged in 1757 by Frederick II, king of Prussia, for refusing to divulge the confession of an army deserter. In 1936 Fr. Felipe Ciscar Puig, a priest of Valencia, was shot to death during the religious persecution of the Spanish Civil War. His crime was that he would not reveal the contents of the confession of another priest-prisoner. Doubtless there are other priests whose names could be added to the list.

In his book *A History of the Seal of Confession*, Fr. Bertrand Kurtscheid quotes Luther answering the question about whether a priest might testify in court: "She [it was a case where a woman had killed a child] did not confess to me, but to the Lord Jesus Christ; since Christ keeps the secret, I also must keep it and unhesitatingly say: I did not hear it; Christ has heard it, so He may say it." Ever since the Middle Ages, the sacramental seal of confession has been and is considered by a great many civil authorities to be inviolable, involving privileged information. One example is the case of Fr. Anthony Kohlmann, whose refusal to reveal the name of a penitent accused of stealing led New York State to pass a law protecting the secrets of the priest in the confessional. Interestingly, the judges in the legal case who ruled in favor of Fr. Kohlmann were Protestant.

This is not to deny that attempts have been made to reverse this very important privilege of priest-penitent confidentiality, even in the United States.

It bears repeating that a direct violation of the seal by a priest results in his automatic excommunication. As the martyrs testify, every priest must be willing to "go to the wall" to protect the seal of confession.

54. What happens to a priest who breaks the seal of confession?

Canon law says that there are two ways to violate the sacramental seal: directly or indirectly. A priest directly violates the seal if he deliberately reveals the identity of the penitent and any part of his or her confession. The violation is indirect if the priest fails in his responsibility such that the penitent's identity and sins are deduced or suspected by another person due to the priest's speech, actions, or inactions. For instance, if a priest tells, even secretly, that "Sue" told a white lie, he has directly violated the seal. Or take this example: suppose "Fr. Peter" tells a group of people that the first confession he ever heard was about adultery. He may think that he has protected the penitent by not revealing the identity. However, suppose someone from that group subsequently hears, in another setting, the actual penitent innocently boast that he was Fr. Peter's first ever penitent. This is a case of at least an indirect violation of the seal. This is why it is extremely poor practice for a priest to mention in a homily even the general types of sins he has been hearing in the confessional.

Direct violations of the sacramental seal result in an automatic excommunication of the priest. Only the Holy See can remit this punishment. Priests who indirectly violate the seal are punished, as the Code says, "according to the gravity of the offence" (*CIC* 1388).

55. What if the penitent needs help communicating with the priest?

If a penitent needs the help of an interpreter, the interpreter is then obligated to keep secret the confession (*CIC* 983.2). This secrecy extends to both words and actions that could betray the penitent. Moreover, this secrecy should be maintained even with regard to things that the priest tells the penitent, since the advice as well as the actual penance itself may indicate the sins of the penitent. Strictly speaking, this secrecy is not referred to as the *seal of confession*. Nevertheless, the seriousness with which the church regards the secrecy of confession is demonstrated by the fact that there are penalties for violating the secrecy, even including excommunication.

H. The Practice of Confession

56. Must a Catholic go to confession?

The church directs that a Catholic is to confess at least once a year (*CCC* 2042). Canon law makes the matter more clear, explaining that each member of the faithful who has reached the age of discretion is obliged to confess his or her serious sins at least once a year (*CIC* 989). The church also directs that every Catholic is to "receive the sacrament of the Eucharist at least during the Easter season" (*CCC* 2042). Again, canon law underscores the matter by stipulating that those who have already received their first

Communion are obliged thereafter to receive Holy Communion at least once a year (*CIC* 920).

It is apparent that these rules offer the bare minimum. The church formulated them as a pastoral initiative in order to guarantee that each Catholic makes prayer and penance a part of his or her life so as to grow in love for God and neighbor (*CCC* 2041). To avoid the sacrament of penance altogether is not healthy for the soul. It is analogous to the person who goes to the doctor only after some life-threatening illness has overtaken him or her. The wise person knows that checkups and visits to the physician are important in order to preserve good health. So it is with this sacramental medicine that is penance. We want to receive the healing grace of God in those moral areas of our lives that are in need of help, lest they lead up to a moment when it is too late. The church is solicitous for all to receive the sacraments frequently. This is because she desires that every person participate in the intimate and life-giving union with Christ.

57. How often should one go to confession?

All Catholics should make frequent use of the sacrament of penance because of its medicinal quality, by which the soul is healed ever more deeply and perfected in charity. The frequency of confession will depend on the spiritual progress of each person. For someone struggling with a particularly pernicious sinful habit, it can be helpful to seek the strength and healing touch of Christ in penance on a weekly basis. The opposite extreme is the case of someone who only goes to confession once a year. It would not be excessive, though, to consider monthly confession as an excellent means for growing in holiness because of the benefits of making a regular confession. This is because most, if not all, of us have a predominant fault or faults. We tend to commit the same sins over and over. It can be discouraging to realize that we continue to fail even after years of trying to overcome some vice or to grow in some virtue. Christ desires to extend his healing power to these areas of our lives. Even if we see no progress in ourselves, we must stand firm in our faith that Christ is indeed pouring his grace into our souls. Often in ways unbeknownst to us, Christ is healing us. Through this sacrament, our past falls are forgiven and we are unburdened of our sins. Furthermore, we are given strengthening grace to resist sin in the future. Frequent confession makes it possible to make great strides in the spiritual life. It would be folly to pass up such an offer from the hand of God himself.

During a question-and-answer period with youngsters about the Holy Eucharist, Pope Benedict XVI was asked if it was necessary to go to confession every time one receives Communion. The pope made two points. First, one is required to go to confession before receiving Communion only after serious sins have been committed. Second, he pointed out the value of going to confession on a regular basis, even if we are always confessing the same sins. Such is the case with our homes and rooms; week in and week out we find the same dirt. It is a matter, always, of starting over again. Otherwise, we don't notice that the dirt builds up until it reaches the point of becoming filthy. So it is with one's soul. If I neglect my soul, being content with myself and failing to work at overcoming sins and failings, I will make no progress. The sacrament of penance is given by our Lord for the cleansing of my soul. It helps to train my conscience and to flourish as a human being who is maturing in the matters of the soul (*Catechesis of his Holiness Benedict XVI*, Saturday, October 5, 2005).

58. Is it better to confess to the same priest or to visit different priests?

Each person is free to choose to confess sins to any priest who is legitimately approved (*CIC* 991; also see Q. 30). Thus, no one may be coerced or obliged in this choice. That being said, there is great value in confessing to the same priest, or what some refer to as having a regular confessor. This is all the more important if the penitent is struggling with some ongoing or persistent moral difficulty or vicious habit. By revealing to the priest in each confession that one or another sin is a chronic difficulty, the priest can give ongoing advice for overcoming the sin. Sometimes a person may be embarrassed about a habitual sin and run from one confessor to another. Often this only exacerbates the problem because the root of the sin remains unhealed; the penitent seeks a "quick fix" rather than dealing with the underlying issues. It would be best for such a person to find a good confessor and stay with him, following his advice carefully.

Another benefit of seeing the same priest regularly for confession is that it helps one to grow in the spiritual life. People hunger for spiritual direction and so a spiritual director, yet, in most cases, seeing a regular confessor affords just the right opportunity to seek advice and help for overcoming sins and faults, as well as help for many types of problems a person may face.

59. May an unbaptized person or a baptized non-Catholic go to confession?

In a certain sense, anyone can go to confession, but not everyone can be absolved. In other words, someone may find his or her way into the confessional of a Catholic church, seeking the counsel of a priest or to unburden his or her soul. While it is not the best time or place for such encounters, it is not unheard of, especially for priests in big cities, or for priests involved in hospital or prison ministry.

A Catholic priest may not absolve the unbaptized, even if sins have been confessed, because the sacrament of penance is only for the remission of sins committed after baptism. Penance simply has no sacramental effect in such a case. The proper initial sacrament is baptism, which both takes away all sins and sets the individual in a filial relationship with God as a result of the divine indwelling.

The situation of the baptized non-Catholic admits of two possibilities. The first and most common is that of the baptized person who is converting to Catholicism. At the end of the time of preparation, usually just before the day set for the person to be received into the church (when the person will be confirmed and receive first Holy Communion), he or she will see a priest for confession. After having examined his or her life in terms of moral failing, the individual is bound to confess all the mortal sins committed since baptism, as well as patterns of venial sins.

The second possibility of the baptized non-Catholic in the confessional is akin to the unbaptized person, that is, the person does not intend to convert to Catholicism but is facing some moral qualm and desires the counsel of a Catholic priest. In this case, since the person is not intending to become Catholic, that is, is not prepared to embrace all that the Catholic Church holds as true and necessary for belief in matters of faith and morals, then the priest would not give absolution. There would be nothing to impede the granting of absolution if it were a case of deathbed conversion with the obvious circumstance that catechetical training is out of the question.

60. If it has been a long time since someone made a confession, how does one start again?

The Holy Spirit is constantly urging us to draw close to the Father through Christ Jesus because he is cleansing Divine Love. The Holy Spirit's mission is to draw us into this union because this is our ultimate good and happiness. Resistance means remaining trapped in the clutches of something that cannot provide true and lasting happiness. Yet, taking that first step, impelled by divine grace, can feel daunting. So, the first thing is to do your best in surrendering to these divine inspirations as soon as possible. Even if you feel trepidation, perhaps because of fear of the unknown, or even apprehension of changing one's life, you should run, not walk, to seek a priest for the sacrament of penance.

No priest would expect a person who has been away from confession for any length of time to remember how to make a good confession, or even a proper examination of conscience. Simply tell the priest at the beginning how long it has been since your last confession. He won't be scandalized because it's his job to help people in this very situation. Just as a doctor is not shocked when very sick people come to see him, so it is with the priest for the soul in need of healing. Tell the priest straight away that you are not even sure how to confess. Undoubtedly, you will already be aware of some of the sins you want to have healed by the grace of this sacrament. The priest will help you with the rest. He may pose questions to help you remember sins not previously confessed that have been forgotten. He may ask for clarification with regard to matters that are unclear, such as the number of times this or that sin has been committed. Don't worry if you can't remember the exact number; simply give the best estimate possible. When it comes time for the Act of Contrition, if you've forgotten it, ask the priest to guide you in it, making a resolve to avoid all sin in the future. Know that the priest before whom you confess is your loving spiritual father.

61. If going to confession is such a good thing, why do people sometimes avoid it?

Confession is making a comeback. If someone avoids confession, there are several different factors at play. One very common obstacle to obtaining the grace of this sacrament is what I call the "***D***" factor: the tricks of the ***d***evil, that is, ***d***espair, ***d***iscouragement, ***d***isgrace, and the like. These are the enemy's weapons. We think that there is no hope, no way out of some sin, because the sin is so grave, because it has become habitual, or because of some other reason. We give up on ourselves because we forget that God is more powerful than any and every evil. We hide from him in shame because we recognize our unworthiness and because we believe the lie that he, too, is ashamed of us. The truth is that Christ has defeated Satan, death, and sin. We can share in the power of that victory by asking for it in the sacraments, and especially in the sacrament of penance. No matter how far away we have wandered, no matter how much we've made a mess of things, no matter how deeply we have fallen in the pit of sin or how dirty we've become,

Christ loves you and me and wants to clean us, heal us, and give us a share in his glory.

Associated with the disgrace is the fear of what the priest will think about the person when he hears the sins. First, going to confession anonymously (with a screen separating priest and penitent) is a great help in dealing with the embarrassment that naturally attends the confession of certain sins. Second, priests are trained to deal with all types of moral failings and will not be shocked to hear whatever you confess. Remember that he takes seriously his role in bringing God's mercy and peace to you. Third, disgrace or shame can be the opportunity to become more humble. St. Thomas Aquinas teaches that sometimes a more abiding grace results from a serious fall because of the greater humility that accompanies the confession. Thus, we should have great confidence in God who is able to bring great good out of our worst evils.

Sometimes not going to confession is the attempt to escape having to face oneself and God, whatever else the excuse may be. It is no easy thing to come to terms with our sinfulness. However, God already knows the sin. He watched it being committed, so it's no surprise to him. Rather, his desire is that a person squarely faces the truth of self-destruction that results from sin so that God can heal the wound and draw each one of us into deeper personal communion with himself. So, all that leaves is the distasteful act of having to own up to sin, rather than running from it or pretending it never happened. Because of this, we find excuses in order to avoid the challenge of conversion and transformation. We forget that grace awaits us, grace that sets us free to live fully and flourishingly the human life, and to begin eternal happiness and peace now. So, we might ask: Why do we avoid peace? It seems silly when we phrase it that way, but that's the reality.

Pope John Paul II wrote about another hindrance to the sacrament of penance: the lack of a sense of sin or a lack of a perception of the myriad ways that the seeds of death are sown by sin. A sense of sin, he says, is linked to a sense of God with which each person is created. The moral conscience can be clouded, dulled by attitudes that disguise their destructive character: secularism (exalting the human being over and against God); errors in the practice of the human sciences, such as psychology (which, at times, portrays sin as normal or even good); ethical relativism (the destruction of moral values); and misinformation fed to our young people through the media and educational systems. So, society loses a sense of sin; even certain factions in the church, too, lose it. The remedy is sound catechetical teaching, vibrant preaching of the truth of divine revelation as handed on through the pope and bishops, and a return to the sacrament of penance (*RP* 18).

Finally, a word to those who stay away from confession because they have had a bad experience talking with a priest, religious sister, or brother, have felt demeaned by a priest in the confessional at some time, or the like. Just as it would be foolish to never consult a doctor in the future because some other doctor or nurse scared or belittled you in the past, so it is with your soul. Be brave and see another priest, one who is kindly, with whom you can share your experience, and ask him to help you practice the sacrament of penance once again.

62. Why must children make their first confession prior to their first Holy Communion?

Baptized children are to receive the sacrament of penance before receiving their first Holy Communion when they have reached the age of reason, or approximately the age of seven. (In exceptional cases, the pastor may judge that a child is ready to receive the sacraments before the age of seven.) One very important reason for this doctrine is the church's concern that children be nourished with Christ's Body and Blood; yet they must first be prepared, not only to know what it is they are receiving, but also, in a way commensurate with their age, to consider and to avoid what may hinder them from receiving this divine gift. St. Paul insists in 1 Corinthians 11:28: "Examine yourselves, and only then eat of the bread and drink of the cup." This is best done in the sacrament of penance, where it is the priest's responsibility to help the young person with an examination of conscience, and where the young person may reveal whatever stands in the way of a deeper friendship with Christ, particularly prior to reception of the Eucharist. If a child is to grow in knowledge and love of Christ, he or she needs the sacraments of penance and the Eucharist just as much as an adult. We know from the gospels that Jesus drew the children to himself. How much, even now, must he desire to heal their sins and free their minds of guilt so as to enjoy his divine love.

Another reason for the necessity of a child to make a first confession prior to first Holy Communion centers on basic human dignity. As one Vatican letter states, the church must protect the right of children to receive the sacrament of penance in preparation for first Holy Communion, lest the child's conscience be violated. Children, as parents know only too well, are quite capable of knowing right from wrong, and at a certain age are able to make reasoned choices for good or for ill. Thus, they must be afforded the right to be healed of any sin that weighs on their conscience.

Finally, the practice of going to confession before receiving Communion will teach the child a lifelong lesson about these sacraments. As the child grows to responsible adulthood, he or she will have been given the gift of knowing that Christ's healing power is always available in the sacrament of penance so that he or she can be received worthily in Communion.

63. Sometimes a parish will offer a special "penitential service" or "reconciliation service," especially during Advent or Lent. What is the difference between individual and communal celebrations of the sacrament of penance?

Typically, people go to confession individually. That is, a person goes alone to the priest for confession and absolution, usually during the published times when he will be sitting in the confessional. Other individuals may be present to do the same, but the priest celebrates the entire sacrament alone with each penitent, from start to finish. A communal celebration, on the other hand, sometimes offered during the seasons of Advent and Lent (in preparation for Christmas and Easter, respectively), is the gathering of a number of people who will pray communally and listen to the Word. Then each person may privately confess his or her sins to one of several priests and receive absolution. Not everyone who attends a communal celebration of the sacrament necessarily needs to confess privately; but since absolution may not be given to a group of people (except in certain emergency situations), neither will that person enjoy the grace of sacramental absolution.

A communal penitential service has this structure: introductory rites that explain to the faithful the order of the service; celebration of the Word of God during which readings from Sacred Scripture are proclaimed; a homily relating to sin, divine mercy, repentance, satisfaction, and the like, given by a deacon, priest, or bishop; a time of silence for reflecting and for making an examination of conscience; a general prayer of confession (similar to the one used at the beginning of Mass); the Lord's Prayer; time for individual confession; and the dismissal.

In addition, it is possible to celebrate nonsacramental rites of penance. These are virtually the same as sacramental celebrations except that, of course, there is neither individual confession of sin nor absolution. It is important for those leading this latter type of penance service to make it clear to those attending that this is not a sacrament. The introduction to *The Rite of Penance* gives reasons why such a service might be desirable:

- to foster the spirit of penance within the Christian community
- to help the faithful to prepare for confession, which can be made individually later at a convenient time
- to help children to gradually form their conscience about sin in human life and about freedom from sin through Christ
- to help catechumens during their conversion

As the introduction goes on to say (*RP* 37), such celebrations are very useful in places where no priest is available for the sacrament and can foster contrition and the desire for the sacrament.

I. Special Circumstances Concerning Penance

64. What happens if a person in mortal sin is near death and can't reach a priest?

First, every effort is to be made to call for a priest at the moment of death in any circumstance, particularly so that the dying person may receive viaticum (Communion). This is not the time to be concerned about disrupting a priest's schedule or sleep. In fact, every Catholic priest is obliged by canon law to hear the confession of anyone in urgent necessity, not just in danger of death. This applies to priests without the faculty to hear confessions or even a dispensed priest (cf. *CIC* 986).

Second, the sacrament of penance is the ordinary means by which someone who has committed a mortal sin is reconciled with God and the church. It can happen, particularly at the moment of death, that some physical or moral obstacle prevents a person from going to confession, "in which case reconciliation may be attained by other means also" (*CIC* 960). Examples of a physical impossibility would include the instance of a life-threatening illness and the penitent is unable to travel to a priest, or a life-threatening accident that happens in a remote location and no priest is available. An example of a moral impossibility includes a justifiable fear of the penitent's harm to him- or herself or to another person if he or she goes to confession.

In the event that a physical or moral obstacle prevents a person from making a sacramental confession, he or she should make a perfect Act of Contrition. The heart of the sacrament of penance is an interior and wholehearted sorrow for sins committed. It is Christ who gave us this necessary sacrament so that we could know with certainty that we have been forgiven. However, God is able to forgive sins even though a person is not able to participate in the sacrament, though not without contrition on the part of the penitent.

65. May a person who has not been absolved of serious sin go to Holy Communion or Mass?

Serious, or mortal, sin involves a break in one's friendship with God. In other words, the communion God desires to share with us is ruptured by one's own doing. Therefore, going to Holy Communion while refusing to be in union with God is absolutely contrary to the meaning and purpose of Holy Communion: sharing in the Body and Blood of Christ, thus becoming united to him in one body (see 1 Cor 10:16–17). Just as no one would dream of sitting down to dinner with a friend whom one has harmed without first making amends, so the person who has offended God must first go to confession before receiving Holy Communion. As St. Paul remarks, "Whoever, therefore, eats the bread or drinks the cup of the Lord in an unworthy manner will be answerable for the body and blood of the Lord" (1 Cor 11:27). Moreover, it is not only God whom we sin against; it is the entire body of Christ, the church. The sacrament of reconciliation restores us to unity with God, but also with the church. For by receiving Holy Communion, we are also asserting that we are proclaiming that we are one with the church and all her members, and in union with all that the church holds and teaches.

It is precisely to be reconciled to the Lord and the church that the sacrament of penance exists. The guidelines for the reception of Holy Communion stipulate that those who wish to receive Communion should not be conscious of having committed grave sin, and that normally recipients should have fasted for one hour. Those conscious of serious sin must go to confession before receiving Communion, except for grave circumstances where no opportunity for confession exists. In this case, the person should make a perfect Act of Contrition and have the intention of confessing the sin as soon as possible (*CIC* 916). Frequent reception of the sacrament of penance is encouraged for all.

The permission to receive in the case where there is a grave reason but no opportunity for confession should not be taken lightly. There must be a grave reason for such reception after mortal sin. Laziness in seeking out the sacrament is not a sufficient reason. A person in such a situation must make a careful interior examination. If he or she has made the effort to go to confession, but was unable, and by not receiving Holy Communion might cause others to wonder about the state of his or her soul, that person should make a sincere Act of Contrition with the firm resolve to see a priest for confession as soon as possible. Nor does the possibility of receiving Communion mean that simply anyone should come forward without first resolving persistent morally problematic situations, such as cohabiting prior to marriage, or being married outside the church.

That being said, we are still under the natural law as well as the command of God to give him due worship, which, for the Catholic, means going to Mass even if one may not receive Holy Communion. Hearing the Word of God proclaimed in the Sacred Scriptures, listening to the homily, being attentive to the prayers, and offering one's own prayers to God: all go a long way to helping each person on the road to salvation. Again, the analogy of illness is helpful: An extremely sick person may not be able to eat for some period of time, but still needs the exchange of communication and love of his or her family. The church is our family who brings us the help of Christ, the Physician of the Soul.

66. Is it true that there are some sins for which absolution is reserved to the Holy See?

The updated *Code of Canon Law* (1983) no longer contains a list of reserved sins, that is, a restriction on the ability of the confessor to absolve particular grave sins. However, there still are offenses to which special penalties are attached, and those penalties may be remitted only by the competent authority in the Holy See. Examples of such offenses include promoting heresy, apostasy, or schism (*CIC* 1364); profaning the Eucharistic species (*CIC* 1367); using physical force against the pope; absolving one's partner in a sin against the sixth commandment (*CIC* 1378, cf. 977); consecrating a bishop without a pontifical mandate (*CIC* 1382); and violating the confessional seal (*CIC* 1388). While these offenses are considered sins and must be brought to the sacrament of penance, the sins normally are not absolved until the confessor has permission from the appropriate authority.

67. What are "penalties" and how are they remitted?

The *Code* distinguishes between medicinal and expiatory penalties (*CIC* 1312). Medicinal penalties, sometimes called censures, include excommunication, interdict, and suspension. The most serious of these is excommunication because it results in a person being forbidden to have any ministerial part in the Eucharist or in any public worship; nor may he or she celebrate any of the sacraments or sacramentals or exercise any office, function, or ministry in the church (*CIC* 1331). Interdict is similar to excommunication but the individual is not prevented from exercising offices and functions in the church (*CIC* 1332). Suspension applies only to clerics (bishops, priests, or deacons) by which some or all of their power of holy orders is forbidden to be exercised (*CIC* 1333). An expiatory penalty deprives a person of particular rights, goods, or faculties, either temporarily or permanently (*CIC* 1336).

Note that the most severe of penalties, excommunication, is called "medicinal." In other words, the church uses excommunication, not to punish someone by damning him or her to hell, but to show that person the seriousness of the sin committed, with the sincere hope that such an extreme measure will cause that person to reconsider his or her state and repent. It is analogous to the action the state takes by quarantining a person with a highly infectious disease, such as TB, who refuses treatment. It is for both the individual's own health, as well as the good of society, that this person be forced into quarantine. Excommunication is a forced "spiritual quarantine" to bring someone to spiritual health through repentance and conversion.

The penalties of excommunication, interdict, and suspension may be remitted when the person has reformed. The penalized person should petition the appropriate authority for the remission of the penalty. This can be done through one's pastor. If it is a matter of unreasonable hardship for the person to wait for the outcome of the normal process by having to remain in the state of sin (see *CIC* 1357), the person may approach a priest in the sacrament of penance and ask for the penalty to be remitted and for absolution. We see here the solicitude of the church so that the repentant person can have peace of mind as the remedy for his or her healing begins. After assigning an appropriate penance (including reparation, if necessary), the confessor will remit the penalty and grant absolution. Additionally, he is to impose upon the penitent the obligation to have recourse to the appropriate authority to receive instructions regarding actions to be taken regarding the penalized sin(s) within one month, lest the original penalty be reinstated.

Typically, the confessor himself acts as the channel of recourse to the Holy See. The priest will know which particular authority he is to contact in Rome. The confessor does this without ever mentioning the penitent's name. The procedure entails that the priest write to the appropriate authority in Rome. In this letter he explains the sin that incurred the penalty and the steps he took with the penitent, and asks for instructions to be given to the penitent. Upon returning to the priest at a time prearranged in the original meeting, the penitent is given whatever instructions were issued by the Roman authority. The penitent is obliged to carry out the instructions.

Let's use an example to clarify. Suppose a man came to me to confess that he desecrated the Eucharist by throwing it into the garbage. He asked to be absolved immediately, not wanting to remain excommunicated. I would remit the excommunication after having assigned him a penance and explaining that further instructions from the Congregation for the Doctrine of the Faith would be forthcoming. I would absolve him of this and all other sins he confessed. Then I would also arrange for the penitent to return at some future time (one month hence) so that I might give him the instructions sent me from Rome. These instructions will tell the penitent what actions he must carry out regarding his sin. This may all be done anonymously, of course, in the confessional.

68. Do priests, nuns, and monks go to confession?

Yes, they do. Even the pope regularly makes use of the sacrament of penance. They do so because of the rich power of the sacrament to help them become perfect in the practice of charity. No one is perfect. We all fall short of the glory of God (cf. Rom 3:23). And we all continually stand in need of the redeeming grace of Jesus Christ.

That seemingly holy people go to confession need not surprise us. In fact, the holier someone is, the more that person is aware that what may appear small to others is no small matter indeed. This is because holiness is much like love. The more one loves the beloved, the greater is the desire to have still-greater union with the beloved. And the deeper one loves, the more he or she will work to root out whatever might cause division of any sort. Lovers are never content to let even the smallest things come between them. So it is with the human soul and God. That's why sin, including venial sin, is abhorrent to the person seeking holiness or union with God and why even the pope goes to confession.

Speaking to her religious sisters about prayer, Mother Teresa told them that confession is quite necessary because it is "humility in action." She preferred to call it the sacrament of love. In it, Jesus removes the divisions in a person's relationship with him.

69. What can pastors do to help their people make frequent use of this sacrament?

All to whom the care of souls is entrusted must provide suitable and realistic opportunities for confession for the faithful under their care who wish to receive the sacrament; that is, individual confession must be made available to the faithful "on days and at times arranged to suit them" (*CIC* 986). Unfortunately, in too many instances it is the case that the hearing of confessions takes place only for about half an hour on a Saturday. While such a schedule may have worked in pre–Vatican II days, the busy contemporary layperson is often otherwise occupied during that small window of opportunity. Another common practice is to make the sacrament available "by appointment." This is a generous offer on the part of the priest and on occasion people will avail themselves of this opportunity. The problem with this, however, is that making an appointment to see a priest face-to-face in order to deal with sins, especially if they are grievous, can be a very frightening and off-putting experience. It also precludes anonymity.

Parishes run by religious-order priests are often staffed with several priests. It makes it easier for them to hear confessions much more frequently. Most often, however, parishes have only their local pastor and he is most likely very busy. Nevertheless, if people are to be healed in this great sacrament, it is up to the pastor to make confession more available.

This may even entail the hearing of confessions on Sundays forty-five minutes prior to the Masses. In such a situation, the priest, having prepared the sanctuary for Mass ahead of time, would be available for confessions for a half hour while still having an opportunity to make final preparations for the Mass. Or the pastor might make the sacrament of penance available on one or more weeknights. It may even entail letting go of other commitments and relaxations in order that his people may have the benefit of regular confession. As Pope Paul VI instructed, "Other works, for lack of time, may have to be postponed or even abandoned, but not the confessional" (*AAS* 70: March 4, 1978).

Another way for the pastor to make penance more available is by using the communal form of celebrating the sacrament, followed by individual confession and absolution. Most often, this is the form used during the seasons of Advent and Lent. It is a particularly auspicious moment for the priest to teach about the healing power of penance and to encourage his people to use the sacrament often.

Simply making himself available for the sacrament, though, will not bring people to unburden themselves of their sins to their priest. As a man of prayer and holiness, the pastor must also take it upon himself to preach and teach about the power of the sacrament of penance, as well as its importance for one to grow in grace, to draw nearer to Jesus Christ, and to have deep intimacy with the Blessed Trinity. St. Paul's words to St. Timothy are apropos:

> Preach the word, be urgent in season and out of season, convince, rebuke, and exhort, be unfailing in patience and in teaching. For the time is coming when people will not endure sound teaching, but having itching ears they will accumulate for themselves teachers to suit

> their own likings, and will turn away from listening to the truth and wander into myths. As for you, always be steady, endure suffering, do the work of an evangelist, fulfill your ministry. (2 Tim 4:2–5; RSV)

It is a fact that priests who know the power of the sacrament of penance in their own lives take great strides to make this opportunity for healing grace available to others.

70. May a priest hear confessions in the church while another priest is celebrating Mass?

Yes, he may, although there is a misconception that this practice is forbidden. Some hold that offering the sacrament of penance during Mass takes away from the focus that should be directed entirely on the Mass itself. On the other hand, many others stress that it is a most opportune time for people to avail themselves of this healing sacrament of repentance, thus becoming even more fit to receive Christ in the Eucharist. Throughout the world, one finds the practice of confessions being heard during Mass, particularly in the cathedrals and churches of larger urban areas where more than one priest is in residence. Religious orders, in particular, are able to do this. For example, St. Mary's in New Haven, Connecticut, staffed by my brother Dominicans, offers the sacrament of penance daily a half hour before the noon Mass, which draws many of the downtown workers. It is often the case that confessions continue to be heard throughout the time of the Mass for people who would otherwise find it difficult to make it to the sacrament.

Far from being forbidden, the practice is allowed and, in some cases, was encouraged by Pope John Paul II. In *Misericordia Dei* ("By the Mercy of God"), the pope reiterated a clarification that the Vatican's Congregation for Divine Worship and the Sacraments had made one year previously. While the preference is to have the sacrament celebrated outside of Mass—although never *within* the Mass itself, as though the Eucharistic Liturgy and penance were one rite—John Paul II recommended that, in addition to being available before Mass, confessions continue to be heard during Mass to accommodate the needs of the faithful, if there are enough priests to do so. Clearly, the pope's pastoral concern was that Catholics have as much access to the sacrament as possible. On the other hand, it is doubtful he intended that people who are at Mass "take time out" of Mass to go to confession when they should be attentive to the Sacred Liturgy. It is likely, rather, that he envisioned the circumstance of confessions not having been completed before Mass, or even the situation of a rather large church, such as St. Peter's in Rome, where Mass is celebrated in one part of the basilica while confessions take place elsewhere.

71. What is an "indulgence"?

The key to understanding what an indulgence is lies in the very unpleasant, but necessary, concept of punishment due to sin (see Q. 19). The good news, however, is that it delights God to pardon us and lift from us the punishments due to sin, if we but ask. In a nutshell, that's what an indulgence is: God "indulging" us, pardoning us. As might be expected, there is a little more to obtaining such a great gift from God than merely wishing for it. Just as someone convicted of a crime must present a special petition to the president of the United States to obtain a pardon or a commutation of a sentence, so it is with the sinner and God.

We saw earlier that a distinction is made between eternal and temporal punishment for sin, and that a person escapes eternal punishment (hell) through sincere contrition in the sacrament of penance. Yet, after this forgiveness, there remains the temporal (noneternal and passing) punishment due to sin. We know, for instance, that the eternal punishment due to the sin of adultery is taken away when the sinner brings this matter to confession, but there are a number of effects with which one must still deal. One such effect is the need for deep healing of the broken trust of the marital bond. Temporal punishment for sin is the purification from all the effects of the sins we commit, in spite of the fact that we may be blind to them.

Every venial sin, too, has its temporal punishment. Think of the hours of exercise needed to burn off the calories gained by immoderate consumption; simply willing the pounds away will not work. Disordered (sinful) attachments to things or people, like extra weight, also require purification.

The reason we need this purification is that the human heart, particularly made for knowing and loving God and each other, is sullied and damaged by sin. All sin makes us gradually more hardened and less able to truly love. Where sin weakens or extinguishes the fires of love, the purification that results from temporal punishment rekindles the flame of divine love, stoking the furnace of our hearts until we are set all afire with divine charity.

Herein is the key: the fires of charity burn away all the debilitating effects of sin. God is love, St. John tells us, and where charity is, there can be no sin. Most simply put, an indulgence is the purification of our hearts from the effects of our sins. It necessarily involves growing in love of God and neighbor. Sometimes this purification is painful but always it makes a person more fully human; it causes one to flourish and brings the reward of union with God.

We should remember, however, that our relationship with God is never just a personal issue, a Jesus-and-me kind of attitude. To be a Christian is to belong to Christ's body, the church. This has implications for obtaining an indulgence, because I can never receive an indulgence on my own. Always, I receive this gift through the church, which the church speaks of as being granted from its "treasury."

There are many ways to obtain an indulgence: through praying, reading scripture, doing good works. Certain conditions are attached to indulgences, such as praying for the pope, and having recently gone to confession and received Holy Communion.

72. What is "scrupulosity" and how does one deal with it?

At a time when moral values are in great decay, one might think of scrupulosity as a thing of the past. Scrupulosity, far from being dead, is the spiritual malady whereby a person goes beyond the norm for examining one's conscience in preparation for going to confession. The mental anxiety of scruples is marked by a sense of fear, dread, extreme worry, or anxiety that some sin or group of sins has not been forgiven by God in the sacrament of penance because of some defect in the sacramental confession on the part of the penitent or the priest. Other instances include anxiety about evil thoughts or transgressions against charity, or even errors in prayers, for example, the priest not properly saying the words of consecration at Mass.

Perhaps the greatest pain of scruples comes from the seeming inability to get rid of the scrupulous thoughts. At times countless hours can be eaten up by the preoccupation with these worries. Even if the scrupulous person arrives at some certain decision about a moral matter, he or she will often begin a reexamination of the matter for fear of having erred or to confirm the conclusion. Still, he or she is not at rest. Scrupulous persons will travel from confessor to confessor in search of relief, but usually end with greater confusion and consternation, feeling greatly misunderstood.

Scrupulosity can spread like a cancer, causing the sufferer to be unable to distinguish a venial from a mortal sin, usually in one or another area of morality, but typically not in all areas of the moral life. In the more severe cases, scrupulosity can take over a person's life. Moreover, rather than finding peace in the sacrament of penance, the scrupulous person either leaves the confessional with consternation and worry or finds something else to worry about very soon after the confession. In certain instances, there may be a psychological difficulty underlying the scruples that may need professional treatment. Priests should study this malady carefully so as to be able to be of greatest possible spiritual assistance to the sufferer who, often enough, does not need a psychologist. This is not to deny, however, that certain persons do need psychological or psychiatric help, especially those whose disorder is clearly obsessive-compulsive or physical.

Probably the worst aspect of scrupulosity is the lack of trust that the sufferer has in any other person's ability to help. Even the priest in whom he or she confides is thought to be untrustworthy, if for no other reason than that the priest is thought to be unable to understand all the ramifications of the issue(s) at stake. Paradoxically, obedient trust is the most important way out of this maze of worries, doubts and fears. The scrupulous person thinks that the only one to be trusted is him- or herself because only he or she knows the intricacies of the sins. Most assuredly, this obstinacy to persist in self-trust will cause the person to sink in the quicksand of his or her unstable mind. The only hope is complete abandonment to God and the confessor/priest. He or she must refuse to go from priest to priest seeking "help."

In her book *The Wisdom of the Saints*, Jill Haak Adels has hit on—and my study and experience confirm this—the first counsel the scrupulous person must "scrupulously" obey (and upon which the confessor must insist): Refuse to consider, even in the smallest way, any sin that you have already confessed in the sacrament of penance.

73. What is "general absolution" and when is it permitted?

General absolution refers to the granting of absolution "in a general manner" (*CIC* 961), that is, to more than one penitent at one time without having first heard each one's confession of sins individually. It is often confused with a communal penitential service. The two are believed to be the same thing, but they are not. General absolution is allowed *only* in emergency situations, which are spelled out by canon law.

The *norm* for the celebration of the sacrament of penance is individual confession, wherein each penitent individually approaches the priest, tells his or her sins, and receives absolution. Even when the sacrament is celebrated communally, for instance, during Advent or Lent, each person is to confess and be absolved individually, either during or after the communal service. As Pope John Paul II pointed out, individual confession is "an inviolable and inalienable right" of the faithful (*RP* 33).

An *exception* to the celebration of this sacrament by individual confession is general absolution. As said above, it is allowed only in emergency situations. One possibility for allowing general absolution is that the danger of death is imminent, but there is no time for the priest(s) to hear individual confessions. One might imagine such a condition existing on the battlefield, during a widespread sickness, or before an impending disaster. Another case—the one that is often misunderstood—entails having a large number of penitents with an insufficient number of priests to hear confessions individually "within a suitable period of time," such that the penitents will be "forced to be deprived of sacramental grace or holy communion through no fault of their own" (*CIC* 961). This situation might be envisioned as happening in a mission territory, where only one priest rarely and briefly passes through a village. Without general absolution, the people would be forced to be without benefit of sacramental grace or Holy Communion.

Such a situation is difficult to imagine in the United States, where people have access to transportation if they need to find a priest in a neighboring locale. Perhaps this is why they mistakenly believe communal penitential services to be the same as general absolution, because there may be "a large number of penitents with an insufficient number of priests," for example, during Holy Week, a feast day, or a pilgrimage. However, this is not to be construed as the case. The people coming to the church are not in imminent danger of death, nor will they suffer the denial of the grace of penance or Holy Communion for a long time. In fact, in these circumstances, the pastor is not permitted to grant general absolution unless he has the express permission of the local bishop.

Additionally, several conditions apply to the penitents when absolution is given in a general manner. First, the penitent must be properly disposed. In other words, the penitent must have the desire to turn from the sin(s) committed against God, with a firm purpose of amending his or her life. Moreover, at the same time the penitent must intend to later confess individually any grave sins that cannot be confessed in the present circumstances (*CIC* 962). The priest has the responsibility to inform the penitent(s) of these conditions, if it is possible for him to do so. If there is time, the priest should also exhort the penitents to make an Act of Contrition.

After having received general absolution under one of the above conditions, the penitent is obliged to later make an individual confession as soon as possible. For example, if general absolution was given because of impending danger of death, and the penitents survive because the danger passes, each is bound to confess any grave sins absolved in general absolution. The same is true of the situation where a priest is rarely present, causing the penitents to go without sacramental grace or Holy Communion. Canon law also makes concessions for the granting of general absolution more than once if the situations warrant it, as described above, even if the penitents have not had the opportunity for individual confession. But we must remember that general absolution is just that: a *concession* granted for particular situations, a *concession* that has qualifications attached to it.

The reason that grave sins absolved by general absolution must later be confessed in individual confession is that the sacrament is built upon the actual confession of sins by each person to a priest. There is no easy way out with grave sin. Just as there is no such thing as generic sin, there is no such thing as generic forgiveness. Each mortal sin must be confessed. General absolution is permitted in drastic situations, but it is not the norm for the way that Christ heals us of the wounds caused by serious sin. As an analogy, when many people have been physically wounded by a bomb, the situation may require certain general measures to be taken because of the limited medical staff and supplies. No one would counsel someone with a serious wound to leave it unexamined for an indefinite period of time once the possibility of specialized treatment was available. So it is with the sacrament of penance. Each serious wound to the soul caused by mortal sin needs to be tended to in the sacrament of penance.

PART THREE

The Sacrament of Anointing of the Sick

A. The Foundations of the Sacrament

74. Why is there a special sacrament for the sick?

As mentioned earlier, Christ gave the sacraments to the church as ways for God's grace to help us reach heaven. These seven ways correspond to the course of events in human life, from birth to death and everything in between. Just as the sacrament of baptism brings the divine life to birth in a person, so the sacrament of the sick aids the person whose bodily strength is waning, even unto death. Death comes for all, and "every illness can make us glimpse death" (*CCC* 1500). What appears as ultimate destruction—to the one who cannot see past the created realm—is actually the necessary doorway to a new and eternal home. Amazingly, even this transition is now brought into God's plan for the sanctification of our entire lives. Prior to the arrival of death, those who suffer illness have this sacrament available to them. "Illness can lead to anguish, self-absorption, sometimes even despair and revolt against God" (*CCC* 1501), but it can also be an instrument of our search for and return to God. I think of the many people I have anointed with this sacrament whose suffering became for them the opportunity to draw near to Christ, leaving behind all that had become an obstacle to union. Moreover, beyond supernatural salvation, this sacrament can aid in the natural healing of the body as well.

While some may think it is enough that Christ came into our world to live, suffer, die, and rise as a man whose human nature is united with his divine Person, clearly Christ did not think so. He wants us to have more than a moral example of how the virtuous should live and die. For he knows that our virtue depends on his grace. We know that being made alive in Christ through baptism is essential for eternal salvation. But we stand in awe knowing that, in his love for us, our Lord desires that even the moments of our sickness and death be sanctified by a special sacrament. He wants us to have a way of uniting our suffering and dying with his passion and death. He wants us to have his divine strength, exemplified in the garden of Gethsemane and the hill of Calvary, to overcome the temptations and assaults of the devil that beset human beings in their moments of greatest weakness so as to arrive at the glory of the resurrection.

When one considers the great upheaval introduced by sin into the order of creation, the damaging of our relationship with God and with one another, and the introduction of disease and death, we can only marvel that God uses these worst moments as opportunities to heal us to the core. "God did not make death, and he does not delight in the death of the living. For he created all things that they might exist," the Book of Wisdom tells us (1:13–14). Whether we are in the grip of sickness or the throes of death, the sacrament of anointing helps us to overcome temptation, sin, and, our last enemy, death. The ultimate aim of the sacrament is to usher us into the presence of God, preparing us for the beatific vision.

75. What is the origin of the sacrament of anointing of the sick?

Even a cursory reading of the gospels shows that one of Christ's favored activities was the healing of all manner of illnesses of the people he encountered. Christ came into the world as a human being to heal us from the ultimate sickness—death. He continues this saving work in the church today through the sacrament of anointing, even as he worked through the apostles both before and after his resurrection. We find in Matthew 10:1 (RSV), for instance, that Jesus gives them "authority over unclean spirits, to cast them out, and to heal every disease and every infirmity" (see also Mark 6:7 and Luke 9:1). These healings, both those done by Christ and those by his apostles, prefigure the sacrament that ultimately derives its power from Christ's passion and resurrection.

The clearest instance in the New Testament of the church's procedure for dealing with someone who is seriously ill is found in the Letter of James, chapter 5. It is set in the context of teaching on the transitory character of this world and the need to pray in the midst of hardship. The current liturgy for the anointing of the sick makes reference to the Letter of James as to how the sick are to be prayed for:

> Is any among you sick? Let him call for the elders of the church, and let them pray over him, anointing him with oil in the name of the Lord; and the prayer of faith will save the sick man, and the Lord will raise him up; and if he has committed sins, he will be forgiven. Therefore confess your sins to one another, and pray for one another, that you may be healed. The prayer of a righteous man has great power in its effects. (Jas 5:14–16, RSV)

The church understands this to mean that it is the priests who are to be called, those who have received authority in the Christian community from the apostles. The anointing with oil harks back to the work of the Twelve in Mark 6:13 (RSV): "And they cast out many demons, and anointed with oil many that were sick and healed them."

Catholics believe that Christ desires his followers and friends to have the grace of healing down through the ages and hence the reason for his giving us this sacrament to be used during times of sickness and at death. As with so many aspects of Christian living, no explicit instruction is given by Christ about how to celebrate the sacraments. Just like the development of the biblical canon (that is, deciding which books were to be included in the Bible), Christ left certain aspects of liturgical and sacramental worship to his body, the church. However, all of these aspects, including those in the sacrament of anointing, have their roots in Sacred Scripture.

References, both explicit and implicit, to the anointing of the sick are found in various writings of the fathers of the church, and the formulas for the blessing of the oil of the sick begin as early as Hippolytus's *Apostolic Tradition* (early third century).

While the Scholastic period (roughly the twelfth and thirteenth centuries) debated whether anointing was more a sacrament of the dying, the Council of Trent, in 1551, decreed that the sacrament "is to be used for the sick, in particular those who are so dangerously ill that they seem to be about to depart from life." This theological trajectory of the understanding of the purpose of anointing is found in the teachings of the Second Vatican Council: It is "not a sacrament for those only who are at the point of death. Hence, as soon as any one of the faithful begins to be in danger of death from sickness or old age, the fitting time for him to receive this sacrament has certainly already arrived" (*SC* 73).

76. What does "extreme unction" mean? Is this the same as "last rites"?

Extreme unction, which means "last anointing" or "final anointing," is the name that was used for this sacrament beginning in the Scholastic era until the present. The *Constitution on the Sacred Liturgy* of the Second Vatican Council (73) taught that a more fitting name for this sacrament is anointing of the sick. The Council wanted to avoid reserving this sacrament exclusively for those whose death was imminent; instead it is the church's wish that the sacrament be widely available.

The way the term *extreme unction* came to be is worth noting. For most of the first millennium of Christianity, anointing was administered to those suffering serious illness with the expectation that, in addition to the healing of sins, physical healing would ensue. By the early part of the second millennium, while theologians generally maintained that bodily healing was one of the effects of the sacrament, they began to focus on the spiritual recovery and to think of anointing as "preparation for the vision of

God." With the stress on the spiritual effects over against bodily healing, the sacrament came to be associated rather exclusively with preparation for death, or, more properly, preparation for heaven. Thus, the title "extreme," or last, anointing.

The Second Vatican Council did not eliminate this name, even though it suggested a different one, referring to "final anointing" (*extrema unctio*) as better called "anointing of the sick" (*SC* 73). Moreover, the Council urged the use of the sacrament for those who are seriously sick, as well as those who are in danger of death. For, when the sacrament is given appropriately at the hour of death, it is, indeed, the "last anointing."

Finally, some people refer to this sacrament as "last rites." It is not inappropriate to use this title, for when the priest is called to the side of the dying person to administer the sacrament of penance, to anoint him or her, and to give viaticum (see Q. 95), as well as giving the apostolic pardon (see Q. 96), he is, in effect, giving the last rites of the church. That is, he is giving the rites or sacraments of the church for the last time. Thus, it is completely fitting to refer to this as "last rites," or even extreme unction. *Pastoral Care of the Sick* (232ff.) gives the order for these rites. In an emergency, when there is insufficient time for this order, penance with absolution is first given, then the apostolic pardon, followed by viaticum and finally anointing.

77. Is it proper to refer to the sacrament of anointing as the "sacrament of healing"?

As we have seen in the preceding responses, the sacrament of anointing most assuredly heals. If, historically, greater emphasis was placed on bodily healing, we know that even today physical healing does occur in some cases after anointing. After all, Christ enjoined his disciples to heal the sick (Matt 10:8). Yet, to expect that this sacrament will without fail bring about physical healing is to misunderstand both the purpose of the anointing of the sick and the meaning of healing. We will deal with the purpose or effects of anointing in a later question. To answer the question at hand, it is better not to refer to anointing as the "sacrament of healing" because the concept of healing tends to conjure up thoughts of physical healing. When a person who is very sick expects the sacrament to restore the body to health, but finds that his or her condition has not improved, the misunderstanding of the healing at work can lead to missing out on God's presence and power, which always brings about what is best for each person.

A second point that needs to be considered is the mysterious will of God. It is always the providential hand of God at work, both in instances of healing and not. It is like one of those great tapestries that used to cover the walls of medieval castles and now hang in museums. The back side of a tapestry is a mishmash of colored threads with little or no discernible pattern or design. But the other side, the side we're *meant* to see, shows a beautiful scene, filled with color, intricately arranged from those little threads by the hand of the weaver, conveying the image in the weaver's mind. Life on earth is like looking at the back side of the tapestry of life woven by God, chaotic as it sometimes appears. We can only see how all the seemingly strange colors and lengths of thread, representing our lives, fit together from the divine perspective. We will simply have to wait to view it all, understand how it all fits together, in heaven. In the meantime, we must remember that God knows exactly what he is doing and that he most definitely cares about even the smallest details of our lives, including our sufferings and joys. The crucifix is a constant reminder that God, and only God, can bring great good out of the worst suffering, for Christ has risen from the dead. St. Paul reminds us that "in everything God works for good with those who love him, who are called according to his purpose" (Rom 8:28, RSV).

Finally, it is helpful to distinguish between "healing" and "cure," as Fr. Christopher Saliga, OP, RN, points out. He writes about the misunderstanding regarding the anointing of the sick when it is thought to be the only alternative left, a sacramental last-ditch effort or placebo-type palliative intervention. A cure, he says, "refers to a patient's scientifically measurable positive response to a therapeutic intervention or a combination of such interventions." Someone with a severe infection may be said to be cured when medical treatment has been successful. "Healing" within the Catholic sphere, however, is something that transcends temporality: It "may or may not involve cure even when cure is fairly holistically defined. This is the case because healing is understood relative to the ultimate reason for which we exist, the face-to-face beatific union with God for all eternity."

Of course, as I said above, it is good to seek to be cured of whatever ails us. In the end, however, Fr. Saliga is correct: "The question for you and me is both simple and frightening: 'Do I trust God enough to pray in union with Jesus in the Garden?' If I do, I am well disposed to receive God's healing (sanctifying) graces via specific sacramental interventions, such as anointing of the sick, graces that may or may not cause curative effects in 'this' situation."

B. The Rite of Anointing

78. For whom is this sacrament intended?

The General Introduction for the anointing of the sick in the *Roman Ritual* (no. 8) says that "great care and concern should be taken to see that those of the faithful whose health is seriously impaired by sickness or old age receive this sacrament." The *faithful* are those who are baptized, typically in the Catholic Church. Priests are to take care to discern what constitutes serious impairment of health. Obviously, this is going to vary from person to person. Priests are to avoid administering the sacrament for lesser illnesses so as not to compromise the integrity of the sacrament. Nevertheless, even canon law insists on pastoral concern: "Pastors of souls and those close to the sick are to take care that the sick are consoled by this sacrament at the appropriate time" (*CIC* 1001). It is also the responsibility of family and friends of the sick person to see to it that he or she receives the sacraments at a fitting time.

Moreover, doctors and nurses should concern themselves in this matter, needing to be concerned about the whole person (body and soul) and not the body only.

Anointing of the sick, as Vatican II made clear, is not only for those who are near death; indeed, "as soon as any one of the faithful begins to be in danger of death from sickness or old age, the fitting time for him [or her] to receive this sacrament has certainly already arrived" (*SC* 73). If the condition worsens, that person may be anointed again. When one who was anointed recovers but suffers from another grave illness, that person may receive this sacrament again. The sacrament may also be repeated for the elderly when an aged person becomes decidedly frail. A person who is about to undergo serious surgery should receive the sacrament of anointing. However, unlike the reception of the Eucharist or going to confession, this sacrament is not to be repeated on a regular basis, for example, on a weekly or monthly basis.

Concerning the minimum age for this sacrament, church law only makes the stipulation that the person receiving the sacrament has reached the age of reason and will be comforted by the sacrament. Generally speaking, the age of reason or the age of discretion is a person seven years old. Thus, a child, baptized as Catholic, who has reached the age of reason and is seriously ill, may be anointed with the sacrament of the sick. It is not necessary to have received the sacrament of confirmation in order to be anointed.

Some wonder whether a person who suffers from mental illness or has a developmental disability is to be anointed. First, every baptized Catholic may be anointed, including those who suffer from mental illness or have developmental disabilities, and are also seriously sick from a physical illness or are near death. Moreover, the General Introduction for the anointing of the sick (53) states that "some types of mental sickness are now classified as serious. Those who are judged to have a serious mental illness and who would be strengthened by the sacrament may be anointed." Naturally, each case needs to be judged on its own merits. In every case, careful consultation with the medical personnel involved is essential. It must be determined whether the administration of the sacrament will be truly helpful as an agent of grace for the patient, depending on the mental disorder. For instance, there are instances when anointing, or even the mere presence of a priest, may cause a worse condition in the mentally ill patient.

The above considerations apply as well to those who are sick or infirm due to old age and, because of it, have lost the use of reason or are mentally incompetent. This is provided, of course, that they would have wanted the sacrament before they became mental incapacitated.

However, anointing is not to be given to a Catholic "who obstinately persists in a manifestly grave sin" (*CIC* 1007). For a seriously ill or dying person who is conscious, the sacrament of penance is the means for being reconciled with God and the church. If such a person refuses to repent, the sacrament of anointing of the sick will have no effect because forgiveness of sins is built on repentance. Thus, it is necessary for the priest first to ascertain, before administering the sacrament, whether the individual will benefit from the sacrament. Just as giving the wrong medicine to a sick person is harmful and potentially fatal, so, too, with the sacraments.

One very common reason why someone may not be eligible for the sacrament of anointing is that he or she is in a marital situation that is at odds with God's teaching on the sacrament of marriage. Another reason may be that the individual is at odds with some tenet of the faith that is essential to Catholicism. Nor may someone who has asked for interventions such as euthanasia or assisted suicide receive the sacrament of anointing without having first repented of such acts. Until these situations are rectified, the sacrament of anointing may not be given. This is not a merely a merciless legalism, devoid of pastoral concern. For, to administer a sacrament, which presumes reconciliation with God and the church, particularly at a time of serious illness, or even impending death, is to mislead a person into thinking that all is well when, in fact, it is not. The most merciful and pastoral act is to deal truthfully and honestly with the situation at hand.

Finally, if there are doubts about whether the sick person has reached the age of reason, or whether the illness merits use of the sacrament, the sacrament should be administered (*CIC* 1005).

79. May a healthy person who anticipates death be anointed?

This question concerns those Catholics who face death for reasons other than serious illness or old age, such as soldiers going into battle or a prisoner about to be executed. The rite of anointing of the sick is intended only for a person whose nearness to death is the result of sickness or infirmity. Thus, a healthy soldier, or a healthy prison inmate, whose death is imminent for reasons other than personal sickness, is not a candidate for this sacrament. Nevertheless, persons facing probable death should most certainly avail themselves of the sacrament of penance and receive the Eucharist.

The case is different, obviously, for a soldier (or any person) who has been seriously wounded or is dying. Such a one should be given the sacrament of anointing before death. The difficulty will be, however, in finding a priest. Spiritual preparedness is necessary prior to entering dangerous situations. This is true for all manner of men and women who risk their lives for the good of others, such as the police, fire fighters, and so forth. This is also a good lesson for every Catholic because we know neither the day nor the hour of our death (see Matt 24:32–51).

80. What is meant by "serious illness"?

As noted earlier, it used to be the case that the concept of serious illness entailed being sick unto death. Certainly this sacrament of anointing is necessary at death. But the church is also concerned that the grace of this sacrament be available to those not at the point of death yet who are very sick. We will say more about this grace later in this book.

Trying to discern what counts as serious illness is not merely a matter of the amount of suffering. For there may be instances when a grave illness causes little pain. Moreover, illnesses interact with each other in different ways in different bodies. So, what might be a minor debilitation for one person could affect another acutely, such as a person already in a very weakened state. One author describes serious illness in terms of "'incapacitation' which impairs the ability to function normally in society.... A serious illness or disorder represents a severe dysfunction of the balance in one's psycho-physiological make-up." I think that the key to interpreting this definition is "severe dysfunction," which connotes something greater than being temporarily laid up or more than having a longer-term but treatable condition, such as the need to wear eyeglasses. A certain prudential judgment will need to be at work when the priest makes the determination, in consultation with the sick person, about whether the sacrament is to be administered. On the one hand, he will want to avoid using the sacrament indiscriminately, but on the other hand, he will want to be sure that the sacrament is widely available to those in need of its divine help.

81. May one who is not baptized or who is a baptized non-Catholic be anointed?

First of all, only someone who is validly baptized may receive the other sacraments. This is because baptism is the beginning of divine life in a person. One must first be made alive in Christ before one is able to receive his other divine gifts, which are the sacraments. Consequently, an unbaptized person may not be anointed. If death is imminent, and the person desires baptism, anyone, even another unbaptized person, may administer an emergency baptism. This is done by pouring water over the head of the person while saying: "I baptize you in the name of the Father, and of the Son, and of the Holy Spirit. Amen."

Second, only Catholics as a rule receive the other sacraments, but extraordinary situations sometimes arise. A validly baptized Christian who is not Catholic may be anointed if all the following conditions are met (see *CIC* 844):

- The person is seriously ill and in danger of death (for reasons other than execution or warfare).
- The person is unable to approach his or her own minister due to some pressing need.
- The person spontaneously asks for the sacrament of his or her own accord.
- The person is convinced of the truth of the Catholic faith in general and is properly disposed.

82. What is involved in the rite of anointing?

The rite of anointing, apart from the other sacraments that may be celebrated in conjunction with it (such as penance and the reception of Holy Communion), essentially involves what we find in the Letter of James (5:14–15): prayer, the laying on of hands, and the anointing with oil. It may take place wherever the sick person is: at home, in the hospital, in a nursing home or other medical facility, in a church, or, in an emergency, at the place of the accident, even a roadside. For the purpose of explaining the full rite as outlined in the ritual, we will consider the case of a person who is seriously ill at home or in a medical institution.

The priest first will want to ascertain from the family or friends, or those attending the person, the condition of the person and his or her spiritual disposition. If family or friends are present, and after the person's confession has been heard privately, the priest will invite them to join in prayer for the sick person. One or another can assist by reading from scripture and responding to the prayers he will offer.

The rite begins with a special greeting, such as "The peace of the Lord be with you always" to which one responds "And also with you." The priest then has the option to sprinkle the sick person with holy water as a sign of the cleansing water of baptism. Then, referring to the exhortation of the apostle James concerning healing (Jas 5:14–15), he invites those present to commend their loved one to the power of Christ.

In a short penitential rite, the priest invites the sick and all attending to ask God's forgiveness. As with the Penitential Rite at Mass, this is not to be confused with the sacrament of penance, which rightly may have just been celebrated. A reading taken from the gospel comes next and the priest may explain the reading in the context of those for whom the sacrament is being celebrated. This is followed by a litany of prayers appealing to God on behalf of the sick person. Then the priest, in silence, lays his hands on the head of the sick person, after which he offers a prayer of thanksgiving for the oil of the sick, which was blessed by the bishop during Holy Week. If the priest does not have the specially blessed oil already with him, it is at this point that he blesses the oil. He next anoints the forehead of the sick person while praying, "Through this holy anointing may the Lord in his love and mercy help you with the grace of the Holy Spirit. Amen." He anoints the sick person's palms while praying, "May the Lord who frees you from sin save you and raise you up. Amen." Other parts of the body may also be anointed, such as the area of pain or injury, but the words of the prayer are not repeated. Next, the priest offers a concluding prayer beseeching God to bestow his healing graces upon his servant. After praying the Lord's Prayer together, the priest blesses the sick and any others present.

In an emergency situation, however, the church allows that anointing both the forehead and hands may not be possible. For example, there may not be time to anoint the hands after the forehead has been anointed. Or, it may not be possible to anoint either the head or hands because of the kind of sickness or injury the person has sustained, or because of the inability to reach that part of the body, such as in an accident. The priest is to use his own hand in the act of anointing some other part of the body when necessary, but may, for a grave reason, use some other instrument. An instance in which this may be necessary is when an infection is such that the priest must wear a medical glove to anoint the body of the sick person, or when extreme repugnance is a reason for avoiding direct contact with the body. "Ordinarily, however, whatever the sick person's condition, the minister will be able to take the same safeguards against infection as do nurses and doctors in the ministry to the sick" (Paulist Press, *New Commentary CIC*, p. 1184).

83. What is the significance of the "laying on of hands" and the use of oil in this sacrament?

The imposition of hands is a primitive rite and has varied significance in the Bible, depending on the context. For instance, it might symbolize ownership of the sacrificial victim by the one offering the sacrifice. When used by Christ and the apostles, it signifies the act of blessing, the bestowal of a divine reality upon another (John L. McKenzie, *Dictionary of the Bible*, p. 385). For instance, we see Jesus blessing the babies and children brought to him (Matt 19:15; Mark 10:16; Luke 18:15). At his ascension, our Lord blessed the apostles with outstretched hands (Luke 24:50). We find numerous instances of Jesus touching the sick with his hands and curing them (Matt 8:3; 8:15; 9:25; 9:29; 20:34; Mark 1:41; 5:23, 41; 6:5; 7:33; 8:23, 25; Luke 4:40; 5:13; 13:13; 22:51). Our Lord instructed the apostles to lay hands on people for healing (Mark 16:18). The practice is found in the apostolic community as part of Paul's healing (Acts 9:12, 17), and again when Paul heals a man (Acts 28:8). Elsewhere we find the laying on of hands associated with the conferral of apostolic authority and power with the ordination of presbyters and deacons. *Pastoral Care of the Sick* (106) explains that by the priest laying hands on a sick person, it shows that the church is directing its concern to this individual. It is both a sign of blessing and of invocation, beseeching the Holy Spirit to come to the aid of this sick person.

Each priest is able to carry with him the oil of the sick, which is blessed in a special rite by the bishop during Holy Week. Interestingly, unlike the blessing of the oil of catechumens and the consecration of the chrism, the ritual calls for this oil to be brought to the altar at the end of the Eucharistic Prayer. (An option is also given whereby the bishop may bless and consecrate the oils just after the Liturgy of the Word.) Thus, we find a connection between the Eucharistic Body and Blood of Christ just made present by the words of consecration and the healing power of Christ imparted to this oil. While the Eucharist is meant for daily spiritual sustenance, the oil in the sacrament of anointing brings the grace of healing and strength particularly when we are most vulnerable as the result of physical illness and frailty. The prayer itself addresses God who sent his Son to heal the world, asking him to send the power of the Holy Spirit into "this soothing ointment" so that it may be a remedy: healing body, soul, and spirit, and delivering all from the diabolical works of the devil. Thus it is that the *Pastoral Care of the Sick* (107) says that anointing with this oil "signifies healing, strengthening, and the presence of the Holy Spirit."

The medicinal use of olive oil goes back to ancient times. It was applied to wounds and bruises and often it was used as an ointment for the entire body. Healing oil is used as a metaphor for God's merciful grace in Isaiah 1:6: "From the sole of the foot even to the head, there is no soundness in it, but bruises and sores and bleeding wounds; they have not been drained, or bound up, or softened with oil." Jesus mentions oil for healing in the parable of the good Samaritan (Luke 10:34). The apostles anointed the sick with oil (Mark 6:13). It is surely this understanding that is the basis for James instructing the priests to anoint with oil when praying over the sick.

84. What if the priest has no specially blessed oil for this sacrament?

It has been the constant practice and teaching of the church that the olive oil used in the anointing of the sick is blessed by the bishop, as was seen above. If olive oil is not available (which may be the case in some parts of the world), the oil of some other plant may be used (Pope Paul VI, *Sacram unctionem infirmorum*). Any other nonvegetable oil is invalid matter.

Nevertheless, the case may arise that the oil blessed by the bishop is not available. Possible scenarios include, but are not necessarily limited to, the natural decomposition of the oil such that it is no longer suitable, running out of the blessed oil, or not having the blessed oil available in an emergency situation. Canon law views such occasions as exceptional (*CIC* 999), using the phrase "in case of necessity." Thus, it does not seem that the simple desire to bless new oil each time the sacrament is celebrated, or some similar liturgical plan, is a matter of necessity.

85. Is a "healing Mass" the same thing as the administration of the sacrament of the sick?

Some parishes celebrate "healing Masses" or healing services. In a certain sense, all Masses are healing because we encounter Jesus Christ, who is truly present in the sacrament of the Eucharist, body and blood, soul and divinity. But the term *healing Mass* can mean different things, depending on the context. In some cases, at some point during the Mass, a priest or layperson lays hands on those seeking healing of one sort or another, even for nonserious illnesses, as well as relationship troubles or psychological difficulties. Often blessed oil is used to anoint the person, although the oil is not the same as that used for the sacrament. This is an abuse of the Mass and can be misleading for those being prayed over, who may think that they are validly receiving another sacrament. While it is laudable and important to pray for people who are burdened with all sorts of nonserious illnesses and other troubles, it is improper to insert rites into the Mass that are not in and of themselves sacraments meant to deepen our worship of God through Jesus Christ, or that may be confused with sacraments. It is most proper to hold these kinds of healing services outside of Mass after clearly explaining, of course, to those participating that the use of oil and the laying on of hands in this context is a sacramental and not a sacrament. Many people are deeply affected by Christ's healing presence in these healing services.

If by "healing Mass" is meant that the sacrament of anointing is celebrated within Mass, it is permissible. The Mass may be for an individual or for a group and usually takes place in a church, but it may be celebrated elsewhere with the permission of the bishop, such as the home of the sick person, or in a hospital. The instruction for the rite of anointing points out that celebrating the sacrament of anointing within Mass is appropriate when there are large gatherings of people, as when a group of the sick make a pilgrimage (*PCS* 132). There are special Mass prayers that are to be offered when this sacrament occurs in the context of the Eucharistic Liturgy. The priest(s) involved should make sure that those to be anointed have "the convenient opportunity" to go to confession prior to the Mass (*PCS* 133).

Of great concern, of course, is that the sacrament of anointing not be abused in these situations by administering it arbitrarily. Not all in attendance are necessarily disposed to receive the sacrament because they do not meet the requirements for reception. It is important to take care that the sacrament be given to those truly in need of it and to instruct people of the importance of the sacrament in times of illness. To simply administer the sacrament to everyone who has any semblance of illness, or simply because they have reached retirement age, is to trivialize this sacrament of healing and rob it of its depth and meaning for those who are beset by serious physical infirmity. "The practice of indiscriminately anointing numbers of people...simply because they are ill or have reached an advanced age is to be avoided" (*PCS* 108). Thus, it is essential that a priest celebrating the sacrament of anointing in the context of a Mass gives a very clear explanation of who may or may not be anointed as well as reasons why this is the case. It might also be helpful to have those to be anointed sit in a special place, such as the front seats of the church. The priest(s) could then speak with each person intending to be anointed to determine if that person should truly receive the sacrament. Those who are thought not to qualify for the sacrament can still be prayed over, simply omitting the anointing with the oil of the sick. Again, in this situation, clear catechesis is required to help the person understand the purpose of the sacrament.

I have heard the complaint that the church's teaching on this matter is too restrictive and is pastorally insensitive. We must recall, however, that not all sacraments are intended for every person at every moment. For example, not all can be or ought to be ordained priests. Again, the sacrament of penance is only for the contrite of heart. Marriage is reserved for those who are properly prepared to vow their lives to each other. Even baptism, the most essential sacrament for salvation, is not simply administered to everyone. Anointing of the sick is to help the sick person bear his or her burden in union with the suffering of Christ for one's own good and for the good of the entire church.

86. Is it necessary to confess mortal sins in the sacrament of penance before receiving the sacrament of anointing?

Normally, a person about to be anointed with the sacrament of the sick should have confessed and received absolution for mortal sins through the sacrament of penance, as the ritual indicates. This is because the sacrament of penance was instituted for the remission of sins, while the sacrament of the anointing of the sick is to give the graces needed in times of serious illness or when a person is dying. The distinction between penance and anointing was clarified when the formula used by the priest to anoint was modified. The medieval form was, "May the Lord forgive you by this holy anointing and his most loving mercy whatever sins you have committed." The revised form (see Q. 82) calls on God's mercy but does not explicitly ask for forgiveness of sins. We should, then, use both the sacrament of penance and the sacrament of anointing in the appropriate circumstances.

Two types of situations may make going to confession impossible, however. In one case, the circumstances may be such that the gravely sick or dying person, who has serious sins to confess, is conscious but either cannot speak or is surrounded by people (one might envision the hospital ER ward, or some other emergency setting). The priest should simply elicit some sign that the individual is sorry for all his or her sins, such as a generic confession, or if the person is unable to speak, a squeeze of the hand or a nod of the head, and then he may give absolution.

In another case, the urgency may be such that it is impossible to elicit even some general sorrow for sins—for example, because the person is being medically treated or is unconscious. In these instances the person should be anointed.

There is an obvious presumption in the latter case, namely, that the person receiving the sacraments has some sorrow (at least attrition) for his or her sins, even if it cannot be outwardly expressed. As we have seen in our discussion about penance, an expression of sorrow is integral to that sacrament. In the sacrament of anointing, on the other hand, no outward expression of even imperfect sorrow is demanded. The church expects, though, that the Catholic implicitly intends to receive the sacrament of the sick (Colman O'Neill, *Meeting Christ in the Sacraments*, p. 288).

87. May a person be anointed more than once?

The sacrament of anointing may be repeated, as we already noted above. There are two possible circumstances for a person to be anointed more than once: if someone is anointed, recovers, and falls ill again, or if the anointed person's condition grows more serious during the same illness. In the first case, the person may fall ill again with the same or a different illness. In the second case, the person's health may seriously worsen, or in the case of old age, the individual may become seriously weakened or debilitated. The decision to anoint is left to the prudential judgment of the priest in consultation with the person, and may include family, friends, and health care personnel. There is no actual limit to the number of times a person may be anointed. Clearly, however, the sacrament is not to be administered indiscriminately.

88. May someone other than a priest administer this sacrament?

While everyone is urged to pray to God for healing, whether for another or for oneself, only a priest may validly confer the sacrament of anointing (see *CIC* 1003). Thus, an ordained deacon or a layperson may not administer the sacrament of anointing. The basis for this is the teaching of St. James to call on the elders of the church for prayer and anointing with oil in the name of the Lord (5:14). The theological reasoning is apparent when we consider, as St. Thomas Aquinas explained, that the priest is ordained to give spiritual gifts to others, be it the Eucharist, the forgiveness of sins, or other sacramental graces. Since the forgiveness of sin is associated with the anointing of the sick, and since only an ordained priest shares in the divine power of forgiveness of sin, only a priest may confer this sacrament (*ST* Supp., q. 31, a.1). Only the priest is able to assure, through penance and anointing, that the sick person is able to receive the Holy Eucharist worthily. Moreover, the priest is deputed to represent the entire church in whose name he prays for the sick person, and not merely in his own name. Only a priest may anoint with the oil of the sick or any other oil.

With that in mind, we should note that the lay faithful can provide valuable assistance. The first way that a layperson helps the sick is simply by being at the side of the sick person who is suffering. It is typically the lay faithful who are in such a position of being present to loved ones who are sick. They are able to offer comforting words as well as to encourage the sick person to seek God's grace by receiving the sacraments. The laity can help the sick to prepare for the reception of the sacraments, particularly to be well disposed for confession. They are able to pray with the sick person and to use sacramentals, such as saying the Rosary or other prayers. Bringing an image of the Lord, our Lady, or one of the saints to the sick room, reading aloud the sick person's favorite Bible passages, or reading the psalms are helpful spiritually for the sick person to join his or her sufferings to Christ's, to bear up in the midst of weakness, and to be open to the myriad graces God wishes to pour forth.

89. May the lay faithful participate in liturgical prayers for healing?

Far from being reserved to priests, the offering of prayers for the healing of the sick is the responsibility of every Christian. Indeed, in the course of the history of Christianity some lay individuals have been given a special gift of grace, or a charism, whereby they are used by God for the miraculous healing of others. St. Paul mentions the gift of healing in 1 Corinthians 12:9; he says that the Holy Spirit gives such gifts, as he chooses, for the common good. Despite this, not everyone is healed through this special gift or even through the most intense prayer. Such healings are the free decision of the Holy Spirit, and this gift is distinct from the sacrament of anointing. The sacrament (indeed, every sacrament) is efficacious, meaning that Christ gave us the sacrament in order to give the sick person all the benefits of healing grace, even if it somehow includes physical healing, while not necessarily having it as its exclusive or primary goal.

It is important to distinguish the cures of miracle-workers from the contemporary so-called charism of healing sometimes found in prayer groups organized for this purpose or at other times takes place at Mass. While prayer meetings organized specifically for praying for healing are acceptable, one must distinguish between liturgical and nonliturgical prayer services. A liturgical service such as the Mass has as its primary purpose to "bring the faithful to recognize in the Eucharist the wonderful presence of Christ and to invite them to a spiritual union with him," and may not be preempted by a secondary goal such as the healing of the sick.

Finally, it should be recognized that the prayer group as a whole, or some part of it such as the leaders, does not possess the charism. It is a gift of God given for various reasons at various times. Again, sometimes people are healed at these gatherings while others are not, depending on the mysterious will of God.

C. The Effects of Anointing of the Sick

90. Why should a sick person receive the sacrament of anointing of the sick?

The first effect of this sacrament is the grace of the Holy Spirit, which helps the person to endure suffering and even to fight against it by strengthening her or him against temptation and against anxiety over death. To put it another way: the grace of this sacrament sanctifies the experience of suffering serious illness. While God never intended such suffering, he has seen fit to make the very sickness, brought into the world as a result of sin, a remedy. This calls to mind the scene in the desert when the chosen people were dying from serpent bites as a result of their sin. The remedy was to gaze upon a bronze replica, lifted on a pole, of the very thing that was destroying them. Just as the serpent became the remedy, so, too, the sacrament of anointing transforms our illness into a remedy that heals the soul, bringing the grace of Christ's suffering and death on the cross into our suffering. His grace strengthens and transforms our suffering and even our death. Because he is risen from the dead, Christ's power infuses us with his peace in the midst of our anxiety and fear and supports our weakness. His grace touches even the interior experiences of discouragement and the temptation to despair. It strengthens us to bear up in the midst of the agonies and pains.

There is another aspect to the strengthening grace of this sacrament, which we often overlook. It is the gift of giving Christ our suffering so that he can make of it something useful for our salvation and the salvation of others. It is not "giving away" in the sense that we will no longer experience the suffering; rather, it is uniting our suffering with his passion. The grace of the sacrament gives the sick person strength; it also gives the sick person the gift of uniting him- or herself to Christ's passion. "Suffering, a consequence of original sin, acquires a new meaning; it becomes a participation in the saving work of Jesus" (*CCC* 1521).

Of all the gifts a Christian might want to give Christ, who would think to pile suffering on him? Yet our suffering united to his is not a burden but a transforming agent, in the same way that his suffering heals us. The sick person's suffering, united to Christ's, transcends the sickroom. What appears, on the surface, a diminishment of life, a wasting away of a person, can, through this sacrament, take on cosmic dimensions. This is why St. Paul could say with every confidence that his sufferings made up what was lacking in the suffering of Christ for the sake of the body, the church (Col 1:24). It is not that Christ needed to suffer more; it is, rather, that Christ desires to suffuse our suffering with his grace to give it immortal value. Thus, we can offer our suffering to Jesus in reparation for our past sins, as well as for the sins of others, for the conversion of others, for the souls in purgatory. Suffering transformed by grace has an inestimable currency with God. With God, no suffering is too small to offer, no conversion too great.

No one who receives the sacrament of anointing does so apart from the body of Christ. When the individual sick person is anointed, and thereby united to the passion and death of Christ, that person is building up the church. On one hand, it is the entire church, including those who have gone on before us, that intercedes for the sick person. But as a member of that one body of Christ, the sick person, transformed by the grace of the sacrament, builds up the church and contributes to its sanctification. Even from the sickbed, the Christian, as a member of the body of Christ, fosters the good of all "for whom the Church suffers and offers herself through Christ to God the Father" (*CCC* 1522). When St. Paul speaks about the unity of the many members of the body of Christ and the various gifts of each member, we do well to remember that we contribute to the building up of the body by the offering of our sufferings for the good of each member of the church (see 1 Cor 12).

91. Does the sacrament of anointing have other effects?

This sacrament offers, if necessary, forgiveness of sins: The Holy Spirit anoints the soul and purifies it of the remains of sin. Purification is not magical, however; the extent to which the Holy Spirit is able to act on the soul depends on the individual's surrender to God and openness to the divine action.

God may use this sacrament to restore the sick person to physical health, if the healing will benefit the sick person's salvation. One might wonder how a physical healing would not always be beneficial. First, as we mentioned in a previous question, there is no physical healing that lasts forever; we all must die. Then we will experience the greatest and most permanent physical healing possible: the resurrected body incapable of suffering or breakdown. Second, not everything that appears to be materially good actually is good for an individual. For example, a poor single mother with young children might pray insistently to win the multimillion dollar lottery. But rolling in wealth is not an automatic recipe for happiness. If it were, every rich person would be very happy, and we know that's not true.

Another grace given by this sacrament is the preparation for making one's final journey to God (see also Q. 95). While this sacrament should be administered as soon as someone is seriously sick (*SC* 73), someone who has not already received the sacrament recently and is at the point of death should be anointed. The reason for this is that anointing the sick at the hour of death completes the sacramental life begun with baptism and strengthened in confirmation, and helps us to be conformed to Christ, even in the moments just before departing to the distant shore of heaven (*CCC* 1525).

D. Special Circumstances Regarding Anointing of the Sick

92. What should the priest do if he is not sure if death has already occurred?

Even with sophisticated medical devices, it can still be difficult to determine whether a patient is alive or dead. Though uncommon, there are modern-day accounts of individuals who were thought to be dead and mistakenly sent to the morgue, only to revive there. Moreover, many times the priest is called to minister the sacraments in places lacking life-sustaining medical equipment. It is probably inevitable that a priest will find himself in the quandary of being called to administer the sacrament of the sick when it is not clear if and when a person has died and the soul has departed the body.

One of the purposes of the sacrament of anointing, as we have seen, is to help the dying person with special graces to endure the death struggle. Thus, the priest will want to take every precaution with the sacrament of anointing. The norms for the sacrament consider the possibility that the priest may be in doubt about whether death has occurred. If he has reason to think that the person is alive, he is instructed to anoint the person conditionally. In this situation the prayer of anointing is begun with the words: "If life is in you..." (*PCS* 263). When in doubt about whether the person is dead, the priest is to administer the sacrament (*CIC* 1005).

It is worth noting that in the case of doubt about death, traditional wisdom suggests that the sacrament be given to aid the dying and even the recently dead person; moral theologians customarily counseled that, if it had not already been administered, the sacrament be given within one-half hour after death when there has been a lengthy illness, and within a few hours after a sudden death.

Finally, it is appropriate for the priest to pray with the dying person, together with the family and friends if possible, using the

Commendation of the Dying found in the sacramental ritual. If it is certain that the person has died, the sacraments are not to be administered. Instead, the *Prayers for the Dead* are offered, again with the family and friends.

93. What happens when a person needs to be anointed but is undergoing emergency treatment and the priest is unable to go near the person?

Each emergency situation has its unique circumstances. Depending on the situation, emergency and medical personnel will oftentimes allow the priest to administer the sacraments if at all possible. On other occasions it may be impossible for the priest to approach the sick or dying person. The priest will pray for the patient. He may impart sacramental absolution, the efficacy of which naturally depends on the individual's openness to the grace of the sacrament. In the case of impending death, the priest may also impart the apostolic pardon. Naturally, the priest will want to offer spiritual comfort to family members of the person being treated. The priest is sometimes called upon, also, to give solace to emergency workers, as happens in major catastrophic events such as 9/11.

94. Does the priest continue to visit the sick and the homebound after anointing them?

Visiting the sick is an especially important work of charity. From the earliest times of the church, Christians have been assiduous in caring for the sick. It is incumbent on family members and friends to visit their loved ones who are confined because of sickness or infirmity. All too often the elderly are left to themselves in nursing homes and their loneliness only increases their suffering. We should not be shy in praying with those whom we visit, for praying with the sick and infirm is not only the responsibility of the clergy. We can make sure that the sick have the Bible, prayer books, rosary beads, and holy images available at their bedside. We can read to them from the scriptures, focusing on passages that are personal favorites or one of the psalms, or recite part or all of the Rosary with them. It is the special duty of family and friends to arrange with the sick person's parish for regular visits from the pastor, who may ask an extraordinary minister of the Eucharist to bring Communion, so that the sick or infirm person may receive the sacraments.

One of the chief roles of the pastor of souls, beyond administering the sacraments, is to visit the sick given to his care. The priest represents not only Christ but also the entire church. His presence at the bedside of the sick strengthens the individual, and even the family, in the midst of suffering. Thus, the sick person may realize Christ's particular love and consolation through the priest. By praying with the patient the priest helps the sick person to remain united with Christ, grow in hope, and know the healing power of Christ.

95. What is "viaticum"?

Viaticum is the title given to Holy Communion when a dying person is receiving it for the last time. The name derives from three Latin words: *via* ("way"), *te* ("you," changed to *ti*,), and *cum* ("with"). Thus, viaticum is the Eucharist "along the way with you" and is given to the dying person to give sustenance for the journey he or she is making from this world into the next. The giving of viaticum to the dying has been a practice since the early church. In fact, it is the principal reason that the Eucharist was first (and still is) reserved in tabernacles, so that it will always be available, especially in emergencies, for those at the point of death, and for all the sick. Ideally and if possible, viaticum should be given in the context of Mass and under both species (the Body and Blood of Christ); this signifies more clearly the "meal" aspect of this sacrament for the journey home. The Precious Blood may be brought as viaticum to the deathbed, where it is administered from a chalice (see *PCS* 26 and 181).

Normally, viaticum is to be administered by the parish priest, his assistant priest(s), chaplains, or religious superiors of clerical religious houses. In fact, these have the duty to do so (*CIC* 911). If no priest is available, a deacon or another member of the faithful, a man or a woman commissioned as an extraordinary minister of the Eucharist, may take viaticum to the sick (*PCS* 29). There is a special prayer to be used when the Eucharist is given as viaticum (*PCS* 207). The minister shows the Eucharist to those present and says either, "Jesus Christ is the food for our journey; he calls us to the heavenly table," or, "This is the bread of life. Taste and see that the Lord is good." Then the usual prayer follows ("Lord, I am not worthy...") and reception of viaticum. Immediately after giving viaticum, the minister says: "May the Lord Jesus Christ protect you and lead you to eternal life," to which the person answers "Amen." These short prayers, unique to Communion as viaticum, very beautifully communicate the divine reality: Jesus comes to accompany the dying person on the journey to heaven. Who could want for a better way to pass over between this life and the next than for the Lord himself to make the journey with us?

All baptized Christians who are able are required to receive viaticum. When death is imminent, the priest should anoint immediately with a single anointing and then give viaticum, although in extreme circumstances he should administer viaticum immediately without the anointing after the sick person has made a sacramental confession, even if it has to be generic (*PCS* 30). If a person has already received Holy Communion and on the same day is in danger of death, he or she may receive Communion as viaticum on that day. If the danger of death persists beyond that day into subsequent days, Communion is to be given once each day. Given that all baptized Christians are bound to receive viaticum, it stands to reason that a baptized non-Catholic who believes all that the church teaches about matters of faith and morals may receive this sacrament. There is nothing in the law, however, that obligates them. Children in danger of death who are able to distinguish the body of Christ from ordinary food and to receive Communion reverently may also receive viaticum (*CIC* 913). Note the lack of any specific age requirement.

96. What is the "apostolic pardon"?

The *apostolic pardon* is a most important blessing granting a plenary indulgence given by a priest in the context of the rites administered to a person in imminent danger of dying. The name derives from the *apostolic blessing* given by the pope in his role as a successor to the apostles. However, priests are delegated to give this blessing when someone is in the last moments of earthly life. The rite calls for the priest to hear the confession of the dying person and give sacramental absolution; afterward he prays one of the forms of the blessing given in *Pastoral Care of the Sick* (243).

The grant of a plenary, or full, indulgence is the complete remission of temporal punishment due to any sins committed. A full remission of temporal punishment means that the recipient of this indulgence, if he or she is properly disposed, will not suffer by having to make amends in purgatory for sins committed; rather he or she can enter immediately upon death into the presence of God to enjoy the beatific vision. We readily see, therefore, the importance of this pardon for the individual who is being sacramentally prepared to pass from this life into eternity. The priest should never refrain from giving this powerful blessing to Christians who are in life-and-death situations. If a priest cannot be present at the moment of death, a person who is properly disposed can still receive the plenary indulgence provided that that person had prayed regularly during his or her lifetime. It is recommended that a crucifix or cross be used when praying for this indulgence; the dying person might hold it if he or she has the strength. Other holy images and blessed objects can be made available at this time as well. If possible, a blessed candle can be lit. This plenary indulgence may be obtained even if another plenary indulgence had already been received that same day.

97. If a person has recently been anointed and is dying, or has died, should a priest still be called?

While the priest may have already given the sacraments of penance and anointing quite recently, he should still be called to the side of the dying person. The priest's presence "shows more clearly that the Christian dies in the communion of the church" (*PCS* 213). At this most important and sacred moment, when a person moves from this world to the next, the priest could have no better place than to be at the side of the dying Christian, assisting him or her with prayer. Even if the person has died, it is helpful for the loved ones to have the priest present to lead them in prayer for the person who just died and give them comfort in the midst of their grief.

98. Are there special prayers in addition to the rites for the dying?

Once the sacraments have been administered and the apostolic pardon imparted, it is essential to remain in prayer at the side of the dying person. Even if the person is not conscious, prayer is always efficacious. Some say that the last of the five senses to stop functioning is hearing, and so it is worthwhile to read passages of Sacred Scripture aloud, as well as the litany of saints and other prayers. In these situations, I encourage the dying person to repeat the names of Jesus and Mary gently, with the attitude of giving his or her soul over to God. In this way, the dying person knows that he or she is not alone in these last moments. Calling upon the saints is a wonderful way to help the person to look forward to seeing the heavenly community in the presence of God. These prayers help to calm any fear or anxiety the person may be experiencing, especially if there is suffering. It sets his or her hope on the resurrection promised by Christ. *Pastoral Care of the Sick* contains several prayers of commendation (see 220). Loved ones may fittingly offer other prayers surrendering the dying person into the hands of God.

99. Are there special prayers once a person has died?

When a priest has arrived too late to administer the sacraments of penance or anointing, he nevertheless offers prayers for the dead person. He may need to explain to the family and friends why he is not able to offer the sacraments, and encourage them to pray for the repose of the soul of the person who has died. The rite suggests that the priest may bless the body by tracing the sign of the cross on the forehead of the body and sprinkle the body with holy water. The body of the dead person is treated reverently because it was the temple of the Holy Spirit. *Pastoral Care of the Sick* suggests a prayer service at the bedside consisting of prayer, a reading from the Sacred Scriptures, the litany of saints, the Lord's Prayer, and a concluding prayer of commendation.

100. What does a priest do when there is a deathbed conversion?

There may be two ways in which a person has a deathbed conversion. The first is when a Catholic who had stopped practicing the faith, or had been away from God for a period of time, realizes that death is near and desires to return to the sacraments. Even if the person becomes unconscious before the priest arrives, he or she may be anointed. The presumption here, of course, is that the dying person expressed the desire to reconcile with God and the church. Whenever anyone attending the dying person learns of such a request, it is imperative that a priest be called immediately.

Likewise, a priest is to be summoned directly when a non-Catholic or an unbaptized person desires to convert in order to receive the sacraments. In such a case, the priest will administer whatever sacraments are lacking: baptism, confirmation, and so forth. If a priest is not available, anyone, even a non-Christian with the intention of doing what the church does, may baptize the dying person. While pouring water, which need not necessarily be blessed, the person says: "I baptize you in the name of the Father, and of the Son, and of the Holy Spirit. Amen." If the sick person recovers, he or she is to receive the necessary catechesis, renouncing all that is in conflict with Christianity (see *PCS* 278).

101. May the older form of the rite of anointing be used?

In 2007 Pope Benedict XVI directed that a pastor may, upon due examination and for the good of souls, give permission for the older form of anointing of the sick as well as for the sacrament of penance (*Summorum Pontificum*). This is worth mentioning because the older form of the rite of anointing permits us to see more deeply the theology of the sacrament.

This sacrament, then referred to as extreme unction, was administered by the priest in time of danger of death due to illness or old age. After the introductory greeting and prayers, the priest anoints the five parts of the body that correspond to the five senses: eyes, ears, nose, mouth, and hands and feet, and prays that the Lord may forgive the sins the dying person has committed by each of the senses and by walking. The concluding prayers ask God to heal the person's ailments and restore him or her to "perfect health inwardly and outwardly."

Clearly the theological focus is on the complete healing of body and soul, and not only on death, though the title of the sacrament tended to highlight the latter. The instruction accompanying the rite teaches that the sacrament was instituted by Christ both as a spiritual remedy and for the health of the body. The church's solicitude for the spiritual comfort of the sick person is demonstrated by surrounding the sick person with its care in the way in which the sacrament is carried out and by urging priests to be present at the sickbed. The priest's role as a doctor of souls is emphasized in the act of anointing various parts of the body with holy oil and praying. Virtually the entire body is anointed, underlining the goodness of all the parts of the body. The priest anoints and prays for the forgiveness of sins committed, asking God to touch, console, and heal what lies beyond the ability of any person to reach. In physical healing, the effects of disease are reversed; this sacrament reverses the effects of past sins. Moreover, just as Christ's body was anointed in preparation for his death by Mary, the sister of Martha and Lazarus (John 12:1–8), so this sacrament consecrates and sanctifies the body and soul and all its sufferings, especially in the case of impending death. Having asked God for the healing of the soul, the rite concludes with a prayer for the restoration of the sick person to complete bodily health, protected by God's power from the devil, and in so doing, strengthening the church.

Like the new form of the rite, the older form calls for the sacraments of penance and Holy Communion to be administered in conjunction with the anointing. The church in every age wants every possible grace to be available to heal, strengthen, and perfect its members, particularly in their weakest moments.

Appendix

A Suggested Form for an Examination of Conscience

This suggested form for an examination of conscience, taken from The Rites of the Catholic Church *may be completed and adapted to meet the needs of different individuals and to follow local usages.*

In an examination of conscience before the sacrament of penance, each individual should ask himself or herself these questions in particular:

1. What is my attitude to the sacrament of penance? Do I sincerely want to be set free from sin, to turn again to God, to begin a new life, and to enter into a deeper friendship with God? Or do I look on it as a burden, to be undertaken as seldom as possible?

2. Did I forget to mention, or deliberately conceal, any grave sins in past confessions?

3. Did I perform the penance I was given? Did I make reparation for any injury to others? Have I tried to put into practice my resolution to lead a better life in keeping with the Gospel?

Each individual should examine his or her life in the light of God's word.

I. The Lord says: "You shall love the Lord your God with your whole heart."

1. Is my heart set on God, so that I really love him above all things and am faithful to his commandments, as a son or a daughter loves a father? Or am I more concerned about the things of this world? Have I a right intention in what I do?

2. God spoke to us in his Son. Is my faith in God firm and secure? Am I wholehearted in accepting the Church's teaching? Have I been careful to grow in my understanding of the faith, to hear God's word, to listen to instructions on the faith, to avoid dangers to faith? Have I been always strong and fearless in professing my faith in God and the Church? Have I been willing to be known as a Christian in private and public life?

3. Have I prayed morning and evening? When I pray, do I really raise my mind and heart to God or is it a matter of words only? Do I offer God my difficulties, my joys, and my sorrows? Do I turn to God in time of temptation?

4. Have I love and reverence for God's name? Have I offended him in blasphemy, swearing falsely, or taking his name in vain? Have I shown disrespect for the Blessed Virgin Mary and the saints?

5. Do I keep Sundays and feast days holy by taking a full part, with attention and devotion, in the liturgy, and especially in the Mass? Have I fulfilled the precept of annual confession and of communion during the Easter season?

6. Are there false gods that I worship by giving them greater attention and deeper trust than I give to God: money, superstition, spiritism, or other occult practices?

II. The Lord says: "Love one another as I have loved you."

1. Have I a genuine love for my neighbors? Or do I use them for my own ends, or do to them what I would not want done to myself? Have I given grave scandal by my words or actions?

2. In my family life, have I contributed to the well-being and happiness of the rest of the family by patience and genuine love? Have I been obedient to parents, showing them proper respect and giving them help in their spiritual and material needs? Have I been careful to give a Christian upbringing to my children, and to help them by good example and by exercising authority as a parent? Have I been faithful to my husband (wife) in my heart and in my relations with others?

3. Do I share my possessions with the less fortunate? Do I do my best to help the victims of oppression, misfortune, and poverty? Or do I look down on my neighbor, especially the poor, the sick, the elderly, strangers, and people of other races?

4. Does my life reflect the mission I received in confirmation? Do I share in the apostolic and charitable works of the Church and in the life of my parish? Have I helped to meet the needs of the Church and of the world and prayed for them: for unity in the Church, for the spread of the Gospel among the nations, for peace and justice, etc.?

5. Am I concerned for the good and prosperity of the human community in which I live, or do I spend my life caring only for myself? Do I share to the best of my ability in the work of promoting justice, morality, harmony, and love in human relations? Have I done my duty as a citizen? Have I paid my taxes?

6. In my work or profession am I just, hard-working, and honest, serving society out of love for others? Have I paid a fair wage to my employees? Have I been faithful to my promises and contracts?

7. Have I obeyed legitimate authority and given it due respect?

8. If I am in a position of responsibility or authority, do I use this for my own advantage or for the good of others, in a spirit of service?

9. Have I been truthful and fair, or have I injured others by deceit, calumny, detraction, rash judgment, or violation of a secret?

10. Have I done violence to others by damage to life or limb, reputation, honor, or material possessions? Have I involved them in loss? Have I been responsible for advising an abortion or procuring one? Have I kept up hatred for others? Am I estranged from others through quarrels, enmity, insults, anger? Have I been guilty of refusing to testify to the innocence of another because of selfishness?

11. Have I stolen the property of others? Have I desired it unjustly and inordinately? Have I damaged it? Have I made restitution of other people's property and made good their loss?

12. If I have been injured, have I been ready to make peace for the love of Christ and to forgive, or do I harbor hatred and the desire for revenge?

III. Christ our Lord says: "Be perfect as your Father is perfect."

1. Where is my life really leading me? Is the hope of eternal life my inspiration? Have I tried to grow in the life of the Spirit through prayer, reading the word of God and meditating on it, receiving the sacraments, self-denial? Have I been anxious to control my vices, my bad inclinations and passions; for example, envy, love of food and drink? Have I been proud and boastful, thinking myself better in the sight of God and despising others as less important than myself? Have I imposed my own will on others, without respecting their freedom and rights?

2. What use have I made of time, of health and strength, of the gifts God has given me to be used like the talents in the Gospel? Do I use them to become more perfect every day? Or have I been lazy and too much given to leisure?

3. Have I been patient in accepting the sorrows and disappointments of life? How have I performed mortification so as to "fill up what is wanting to the sufferings of Christ"? Have I kept the precept of fasting and abstinence?

4. Have I kept my senses and my whole body pure and chaste as a temple of the Holy Spirit consecrated for resurrection and glory, and as a sign of God's faithful love for men and women, a sign that is seen most perfectly in the sacrament of matrimony? Have I dishonored my body by fornication, impurity, unworthy conversation or thoughts, evil desires, or actions? Have I given in to sensuality? Have I indulged in reading, conversation, shows, and entertainments that offend against Christian and human decency? Have I encouraged others to sin by my own failure to maintain these standards? Have I been faithful to the moral law in my married life?

5. Have I gone against my conscience out of fear or hypocrisy?

6. Have I always tried to act in the true freedom of the sons and daughters of God according to the law of the Spirit, or am I the slave of forces within me?

Appendix III PENANCE 461–65. From *The Rites of the Catholic Church as Revised by Decree of the Second Vatican Ecumenical Council and Published by Authority of Pope Paul VI.* Study Edition. New York: Pueblo Publishing, 1976, 1983. Rite of Penance translation © 1974, ICEL.

Notes

Each note corresponds to the number of its Question and Answer.

Q. 1. Hugh of St. Victor, *On the Sacraments of the Christian Faith (De Sacramentis)*, trans. Roy J. Deferrari (Cambridge, MA: The Medieval Academy of America, 1951), 162–63.

Q. 12. The *Catechism* defines sin as "an offense against reason, truth, and right conscience" and "failure in genuine love for God and neighbor caused by a perverse attachment to certain goods." Sin wounds human nature and injures human solidarity (*CCC* 1849).

Q. 43. Canon law also mandates that a priest may not absolve an accomplice with whom he has been involved in a sin against the sixth commandment.

Q. 45. See *The Canon Law, Letter and Spirit: A Practical Guide to the Code of Canon Law*, ed. The Canon Law Society of Great Britain and Ireland (London: Geoffrey Chapman 1995), 799.

Q. 48. Fr. Romano Guardini, *The Living God* (Manchester, NH: Sophia Institute Press), 71–72; also Fyodor Dostoevsky, *The Brothers Karamazov*, trans. Richard Pevear and Larissa Volokhonsky (New York: Everyman's Library, 1990), 52.

Q. 53. Fr. Bertrand Kurtscheid, *A History of the Seal of Confession* (St. Louis, MO: Herder, 1927), 315.

Q. 54. See *The Canon Law, Letter and Spirit: A Practical Guide to the Code of Canon Law*, ed. The Canon Law Society of Great Britain and Ireland (London: Geoffrey Chapman, 1995), 799.

Q. 62. For those who would like to read the official church documents, they are: *CIC* 914; Pope Pius X, *Quam Singulari*, 1910; Sacred Congregations of the Sacraments and for the Clergy, *Sanctus Pontifex* ("Confession Before First Communion"), May 24, 1973; Congregation for Divine Worship, *Redemptionis Sacramentum*, 2004, no. 87; Cardinal James Knox and Cardinal John Wright, A Letter from the Vatican: First Penance, First Communion, March 31, 1977.

Q. 64. Cf. *The Canon Law, Letter and Spirit: A Practical Guide to the Code of Canon Law*, ed. The Canon Law Society of Great Britain and Ireland (London: Geoffrey Chapman 1995), 525.

Q. 65. See the website of the United States Conference of Catholic Bishops: http://www.usccb.org/liturgy/current/intercom.shtml.

Q. 68. Mother Teresa, *Total Surrender*, ed. Brother Angelo Devananda (Ann Arbor, MI: Servant Books, 1985), 100–101.

Q. 71. Though many more indulgences exist than are listed in it, an excellent resource for the church's teaching on indulgences and a list of their various kinds is *Manual of Indulgences: Norms and Grants*, published by the Apostolic Penitentiary (Washington, DC: USCCB, 1999).

Q. 72. Jill Haak Adels, *The Wisdom of the Saints: An Anthology* (New York: Oxford University Press, 1989). Another fine resource for dealing with this issue, for both the scrupulous person as well as the priest, is the book by Fr. Thomas M. Santa, CSsR, *Understanding Scrupulosity: Helpful Answers for Those Who Experience Nagging Questions and Doubts* (Liguori, MO: Liguori Publications, 1999). Although this next book is out of print and thus more difficult to find, I also recommend to priests the section on scruples in Adolphe Tanquerey, *The Spiritual Life: A Treatise on Ascetical and Mystical Theology* (St. Benedict Press, 2001).

Q. 75. Norman Tanner, SJ, *Decrees of the Ecumenical Councils*, vol. 2 (Washington, DC: Georgetown University Press, 1990), 711. Vatican II's *Constitution on the Sacred Liturgy* can be found on the Vatican website at http://www.vatican.va/archive/hist_councils/ii_vatican_council/documents/vat-ii_const_19631204_sacrosanctum-concilium_en.html.

Q. 76. For more on the history of this sacrament, see Bernhard Poschmann, *Penance and the Anointing of the Sick* (New York: Herder and Herder, 1964).

Q. 77. See the Catholic Bioethics Channel at http://bioethics.catholicexchange.com/2008/08/18/79.

Q. 78. A very excellent source to consult is Fr. Norman Autton's *The Pastoral Care of the Mentally Ill* (London: SPCK, 1969).

Q. 80. The description of serious illness is from John C. Kasza, *Understanding Sacramental Healing: Anointing and Viaticum* (Chicago: Hillenbrand Books, 2007), 10.

Q. 86. Pope Paul VI, *Sacram unctionem infirmorum*, 1972. The pope, in the same document, explained the change in this way: "We have thought fit to modify the sacramental form in such a way that, by reflecting the words of James, it may better express the effects of the sacrament." http://www.vatican.va/holy_father/paul_vi/apost_constitutions/documents/hf_p-vi_apc_19721130_sacram-unctionem_en.html; also Colman O'Neill, *Meeting Christ in the Sacraments* (Staten Island, NY: Alba House, 1964), 288.

Q. 88. See the 1997 instruction "On Certain Questions Regarding the Collaboration of the Non-ordained Faithful in the Sacred Ministry of Priest." http://www.vatican.va/roman_curia/congregations/cclergy/documents/rc_con_interdic_doc_15081997_en.html.

Q. 89. On prayers for healing, see *Instruction on Prayers for Healing* (September 14, 2000) from the Congregation for the Doctrine of the Faith. http://www.vatican.va/roman_curia/congregations/cfaith/documents/rc_con_cfaith_doc_20001123_istruzione_en.html.

Q. 101. For the older form of the rite, see *The Roman Ritual*, vol. 1: *The Sacraments and Processions*, translated and edited by Philip T. Weller (Milwaukee: The Bruce Publishing Company, 1950). The pope's directive is in the same document, *Summorum Pontificum*, in which he gave permission for the older form of the Mass in use in 1962 and before to be used.

For Further Reading

Autton, Norman. *The Pastoral Care of the Mentally Ill.* London: SPCK, 1969.

Baur, Benedict. *Frequent Confession: Its Place in the Spiritual Life.* Dublin: Four Courts Press, 1984.

Coffey, David M. *The Sacrament of Reconciliation.* Collegeville, MN: Liturgical Press, 2001.

Communion of the Sick. Collegeville, MN: Liturgical Press, 1984. Contains the official texts for use by ministers of Communion who bring the Eucharist to the sick.

Dubruiel, Michael. *A Pocket Guide to Confession.* Huntington, IN: Our Sunday Visitor Publications, 2007.

"Form of Examination of Conscience." Collegeville, MN: Liturgical Press, 1999. A six-page leaflet that prepares the penitent through a series of questions to help reflect on the state of his or her conscience.

Glen, Genevieve, OSB, ed. *Recovering the Riches of Anointing: A Study of the Sacrament of the Sick.* Collegeville, MN: Liturgical Press, 2002.

"A Guide to Confession." Published by Knights of Columbus, 2007.

Gusmer, Charles W. *And You Visited Me: Sacramental Ministry to the Sick.* Revised edition. Collegeville, MN: Liturgical Press, 1990.

John Paul II. *Dives in Misericordia* ("On the Mercy of God"). Encyclical Letter. http://www.vatican.va/edocs/ENG0215/_INDEX.HTM.

———. *Familiaris Consortio* ("On the Role of the Christian Family in the Modern World"). Apostolic Exhortation. November 1981. http://www.vatican.va/holy_father/john_paul_ii/apost_

exhortations/documents/hf_jp-ii_exh_19811122_familiaris-consortio_en.html.

———. *Misericordia Dei* ("On Certain Aspects of the Celebration of the Sacrament of Penance"). Apostolic Letter. April 7, 2002. http://www.vatican.va/holy_father/john_paul_ii/motu_proprio/documents/hf_jp-ii_motu-proprio_20020502_misericordia-dei_en.html.

———. "The Pastoral Care of the Divorced and Remarried." http://www.ewtn.com/library/PAPALDOC/JP970124.htm.

———. *Reconciliatio et Paenitentia* ("On Reconciliation and Penance in the Mission of the Church Today"). Postsynodal Apostolic Exhortation. http://www.vatican.va/holy_father/john_paul_ii/apost_exhortations/documents/hf_jp-ii_exh_02121984_reconciliatio-et-paenitentia_en.html.

Kasza, John C. *Understanding Sacramental Healing: Anointing and Viaticum*. Chicago: Hillenbrand Books, 2007.

Klein, Gregory, OCarm, and Robert Wolfe, OCarm. *Pastoral Foundations of the Sacraments: A Catholic Perspective*. New York/Mahwah, NJ: Paulist Press, 1998.

Larson-Miller, Lizette. *The Sacrament of Anointing of the Sick*. Collegeville, MN: Liturgical Press, 2005.

Manual for the Penitent. Collegeville, MN: Liturgical Press, 1992. Contains prayers of preparation, an examination of conscience, a rite for reconciliation of individual penitents, a communal rite with individual confession and absolution, and prayers of thanksgiving for reconciliation.

Manual of Indulgences: Norms and Grants. Apostolic Penitentiary. Washington, DC: USCCB, 1999.

Mick, Lawrence E. *Anointing*. Understanding the Sacraments. Collegeville, MN: Liturgical Press, 2007.

———. *Penance*. Understanding the Sacraments. Collegeville, MN: Liturgical Press, 2007.

O'Neill, Colman, OP. *Meeting Christ in the Sacraments*. Staten Island, NY: Alba House, 1964.

Pastoral Care of the Sick: Rites of Anointing and Viaticum. Prepared by the International Commission on English in the Liturgy. New York: Catholic Book Publishing Co., 1985.

Pontifical Council for the Family. "*Vademecum* for Confessors Concerning Some Aspects of the Morality of Conjugal Life." February 12, 1997. http://www.vatican.va/roman_curia/pontifical_councils/family/documents/rc_pc_family_doc_12021997_vademecum_en.html.

Poschmann, Bernhard. *Penance and the Anointing of the Sick.* Trans. Francis Courtney. New York: Herder and Herder, 1964.

Santa, Thomas M. *Understanding Scrupulosity.* Liguori, MO: Liguori Publications, 1999.

Stafford, Cardinal James Francis. "Address on the Sacraments of Healing: Reconciliation and Anointing." September 21, 2006. http://www.vatican.va/roman_curia/tribunals/apost_penit/documents/rc_trib_appen_doc_20060921_stafford-reconciliation_en.html.

Stasiak, Kurt, OSB. *A Confessor's Handbook.* Mahwah, NJ: Paulist Press, 1999.

von Speyr, Adrienne. *Confession.* San Francisco: Ignatius Press, 1985.

Walsh, Christopher J. *The Untapped Power of the Sacrament of Penance: A Priest's View.* Cincinnati: Servant Press, 2005.

Index